sensible keto

*MAKE
THE FOODS
YOU LOVE*

*PART OF YOUR
FOREVER LIFE*

kimber chin

Cover Design by 100Covers.com
Interior Design by FormattedBooks.com

ISBN-13: 978-1-953081-01-8

Hello!

What would it be like to feel energized, happy, and satisfied while following an eating plan? What if your next diet included eating pizza, tacos, and brownies? Eating keto is popular because it's delicious and effective. It's also easier than it looks!

If you've tried keto before and didn't have a good time, then it's time to rethink how you do keto. After a lifetime of being a foodie and four years as a low-carb cook, I have mastered the art of eating well while eating keto. Together, we will answer questions like:

- Can I cheat and still stay keto?
- What about heart disease from all that fat?
- How can I do this if my family doesn't want to eat this way?
- What about travel and special occasions?
- What cocktails do you recommend?
- Have you seen my car keys? Oh wait, that's me not you.

Sometimes I feel organized and I accomplish keto as designed, and other times I just need to eat. Sometimes I cook with grass-fed beef and organic veggies, and sometimes I make a last-minute dash for fast food on the way to my next appointment. Keeping to my keto ways and being sensible about each situation in life as it unfolds is what matters.

By being realistic about the changing nature of each day and the value of delicious favorite foods as contributors to our overall joy level, we can adopt a sustainable approach for a lifetime of health and joy!

-Kimber

I would like to dedicate this book to the following people:

My life partner Alan
Thank you for making this dream a reality and always being in my corner. You always encourage me, despite my never-ending ideas for upsiding life, and I love you for it!

My mother
You always wanted something more for Tom and me, and you worked so hard to set us up for success in America. I am so grateful for your time, love, and support through thick and thin, and most of all I am grateful for your enduring friendship.

My father
Everyone needs a safety net, and you've come through for me in so many key moments of my life. Thank you for taking me camping, crabbing, and fishing, teaching me how to fix things in home and business, and to never settle for anything less than the thinnest rim on my martini glass.

My kids
Dani, your wisdom, beauty (inside and out), and grace in movement bring me to tears every time. Heartfelt gratitude for your magnificent illustrations for this book! Josh, your inquisitive mind and quickness with numbers are amazing. To both of you, thank you for the life les-

sons, hugs, and smiles, and always remember I love you more than words can say.

Nancy

Lastly, I'd like to dedicate this book to my dear friend Nancy Jennings, who didn't get the chance for a long life after battling cancer. People think keto is about weight loss, but for me keto is about starving cancer. Until I met Nancy, I ate whatever I wanted and didn't think much about it. While she and I battled cancer side by side, she focused on healing modalities, good food, friends, and living large, while I sat back and marveled, just getting by. Because of her, we were featured in the PR campaign for the Avon Walk, with our faces in major magazines, billboards, and bus stops all over the US, we were included in the book *Why We Walk*, we did the Avon Walk during active treatment two years in a row, and in her passing she gave me an art piece that taught me the good it does to a soul to curate a personal art collection. She triggered me to live large, to shed fear, and to go for all things. Nancy, I wrote a book! Thank you for showing me the courage to live large.

CONTENTS

While you are reading this book, you'll want to take notes, and who has time for that?! Let's be sensible! My latest tips, favorite brands, and quick meal ideas are dynamic and always changing. So head on over to ketokimber.com and download your free copy! You'll be glad you did!

To download your FREE copy, go to https://www.ketokimber.com

We are constantly bombarded with so many dos and don'ts when venturing into healthy eating, along with so much contradiction. Who and what can we possibly look toward as offering sound knowledge? Many books focus on "diet," which if you look at it carefully has the word die in it. Meaning part of you would have to die in order to get the results you may be looking for. With this book you have the flexibility to get amazing results AND nobody has to die!

Happily, perfection is not the end goal here. Because we are all metabolically different, with different environments, ages, and genders, there is no "perfect" knowledge that fits everyone. That is precisely why this story offers such a good balance. As long as you are monitoring your personal results, your choices around eating habits can be adjusted and tailored to what you like to eat.

In the next pages, you will learn about eating joyfully: how to manage eating when you travel, what to do when you are invited to someone's home, or how to cope when you are scrambling to get food on the table for your own family and don't have a plan.

The primary reason for supporting this approach is our collective alignment of values and the belief of "doing the best you can with what you have." Kimber offers a fresh, flexible approach to habits and what I call "inward goal setting." Inward goal setting positions the individual to become the identity first, then adopt characteristics that contribute to becoming the kind of person who exchanges old eating habits for easy-to-follow new ones.

As you read, take notes to become more aware of when those old cravings approach and what to do to replace them with tasty and healthy choices. Remember, it's more about actively choosing to eat responsibly than it is about "perfect" eating.

Robert Lee Smith, M.N.L.P. M.C.H.
Founder of Becoming Whole Therapy, the
Journey to Peak Mental Performance
www.becomingwholetherapy.com

Positive Thinking = The Beginning
Positive Believing = The Middle
Positive Knowing = The End

INTRODUCTION: STARVING CANCER

I love to eat. I especially love to eat really tasty food! Before low-carbing, I was that person who didn't just eat ice cream, it had to be a unique, handcrafted one. Or, if I wanted a sandwich it had to be from that amazing deli, not just a junky, pre-made soggy thing. I always joked that I should have trained to become a sommelier or a fine dining restaurant reviewer because I love what I love and can dissect a meal in an instant (needs more salt, or a squirt of lemon would brighten this up, or they should have browned the components for more umami).

After becoming a low-carber, I went through a period of intense frustration. Everything I knew about how to enjoy food got turned on its head. How was I supposed to cook for me as a low-carber and the rest of my nonparticipating family? How do I go out with friends without feeling left out of the delicious stuff? Why can't I make food that is low carb taste as delicious as my conventional cooking? Why is my baking prowess suddenly flopsville?

Life is too short to not enjoy food. Food is the landscape for social gatherings, it's a source of daily joy, and for me it's sometimes the highlight of my day to just sit with something yummy and relax.

Are you hungry for what you love? Are you wondering if you can stick this out and make it a lifestyle change?

After four years of this, I assure you, I've got the hookup. There are so many tricks that make this way of eating easier than ever. After years of helping friends get through these same knotholes, I've decided to create this book to share my ideas and tips with all of you.

As you will learn in a bit, I had a huge why for eating low carb. My story applies to you, too. I'd like to see everyone eat fewer carbs for health reasons. But I didn't survive what I survived to eat mediocre food. I love to eat, and I always will! Want to eat yummy with me? Then let's do this. Read on!

Why this matters

Have you ever watched how excited kids get when you say it's time for a snack? I love the word "snack." It conjures up that super delicious moment right before the dopamine hit that says, "Aw yeah, that was GOOOOD."

It matters to me to eat things I like, to enjoy that new farm-to-fork place, to visit places and try what they are known for. It also matters to me to be healthy and to eat along the edges of the grocery store. I want to be that person who watches all the food documentaries and takes a stand against mainstream Big Food, feedlots, and mass consumption, but the truth for me has lain somewhere in the middle. I applaud my friends who go vegan and reduce their footprint and may someday go there myself, but right now I'm a single working mama who for the umpteenth time is running late and can't find her car keys.

There's a story behind how I wound up in the middle.

When I was thirty-four, I had just had my second child, Josh, and he didn't to want to nurse on my "good" side. Considering my daughter Dani had no issues with nursing, I had it checked and was reassured it was just a benign lump called a fibroadenoma. A few months earlier, on a sunny day in the Hewlett Packard Roseville parking lot, my dear friend Kristin had walked me out on my last day before maternity leave, and she encouraged me to question the diagnosis, to be more aggressive. I remember laughing her off.

That December, I found a golf ball-sized lump under my arm and was annoyed because I was just heading out to my annual weeklong girls' ski trip to Mammoth Lakes.

Annoyance turned to utter disbelief when I was diagnosed with late-stage, aggressive breast cancer that had spread to create that lump under my arm. I didn't even understand most of what was being said to me. And instead of heading out on my trip, I was heading into emergency surgery to remove body parts.

Just so you know, when a hospital system mobilizes quickly around you with urgency and requests to see you immediately after diagnostic tests, that is what my friend Ernest would say is not a good sign.

The surgery was scheduled within the week, which is another way you know things are serious. The other disconcerting part of a cancer diagnosis is how the news unwinds over time due to the timing of different tests. Each day I'd get a call with compounding amounts of new and unfavorable news.

I didn't know anything about breast cancer, so I just followed the recommendations and jumped in. I had two young kids and a 20 percent chance of survival. I was set on being in the 20 percent!

I never did take that ski trip and instead started a multiyear journey of surgeries, PICC lines, chemotherapy, radiation, and more. I lost my hair, I lost enjoying Josh's babyhood, and most of all I lost myself. It turns out the journey is not just the treatment but also the mental journey back to "well." It caused me to question whether I was living my most radiant life.

I could tell I wasn't living my most radiant life, but I didn't think I could make it better. In fact, I wanted other people to make it better for me.

Once I started to feel better, I was hard-core about toxins in my home environment, only eating a certain way, not using deodorant, and juicing. Everything had to be organic. Everything had to be nontoxic. Everything had to be thoroughly evaluated for safety. Through the years I also tried raw vegan, paleo, and gluten-free ways of eating.

I believe all methods are good for whoever chooses them, but here is why I decided to find my middle ground and go low carb with a sensible twist.

Four years ago, I was lying in the dark waiting for radioactive glucose to flow through my IV because I was in for a PET scan. The idea behind a PET scan is that cancer cells uptake the sugar, and then when they put me in a machine it will be what lights up first.

As I lay there, I thought to myself, if this is the way they track my cancer, then why on earth would I eat sugar anymore?!

I left that day determined not only to not eat sugar but also to not eat high-glucose foods like pasta and bread. I knew from my days as a backpacker and from my 100k bike rides that bonking (i.e., hitting the wall) occurs when your body is asking for more fuel faster than your cells can convert it, and I wanted to just stay in fat-burning mode all the time.

And it turned out, being hard-core about everything in my environment was sucking the joy out of me. Although I could still keep all those things out of my home and out of my body, the process of reading labels and watching everything was stealing the joy from my remaining days. After surviving cancer, I decided I wanted to really live, and to live without the additional pressure of trying to live perfectly.

Now, I think about what I'm craving at any particular time and challenge myself to make a dish to satisfy the craving. I eat things that fill me up and taste fab, like a hearty stew on a cold evening, chili with all the fixings, cakes and cookies, taco night, a truly creative salad, and fun small plates at my favorite restaurant. I can indulge my inner child, eat what delights me, and most of all, eat SNACKS. I count carbs and not calories. Sound yummy?

Then let's do this. No suffering! I didn't survive cancer to then skip out on the fun of eating. So let's make eating fun again. Let me show you how.

WHAT IS SENSIBLE KETO?

I. Why Sensible Keto is worth trying

When I first started my low-carb journey, keto was a relatively obscure phrase, and the number of companies serving this category was small. I made most of my treats from scratch, usually by trial and error, and had to hunt for ingredients not at my regular grocery store but in far-flung health food stores and by ordering online.

Now, it's such a craze that honestly, not everything out there marked keto is truly low carb or good for you. So let me be super clear about what I mean by Sensible Keto.

Sensible keto is a way of eating in which I eat low carb enough that my body uses ketones for fuel, ideally burning stored or consumed fat, and not storing the things I eat as fat. I shoot for low carb, medium protein, and high fat, but not by eating bacon and eggs all the time. For example, 70%–80% of calories from healthful fats, and the remainder from protein and carbs, keeping carbs below 30 net grams a day.

I look for healthful fat sources like avocados and pastured meat and dairy, but if I'm traveling I take what I can find as long as it's low carb, even if that means ganky mainstream eggs and bacon. I make things from scratch when I can and use prepackaged foods creatively when I can't. That's the sensible part.

The reason it's worth trying is that I don't know of many eating plans out there that have such a wide range of delicious choices. The upside of eating keto is you absolutely can make it so you don't feel deprived, and for a cancer survivor, that is a big deal. You don't beat cancer just to live a meager food life.

You get to eat a lot of delicious foods, and there is light at the end of the tunnel, in that if you do it long enough, you can weave back in things you thought you'd given up forever. Mine are red velvet cupcakes and fried salty things like skinny sweet potato french fries or kettle chips. I know, embarrassing.

Although I started eating keto for anticancer reasons, some happy additional outcomes were that I lost my postmenopausal tummy tire, eliminated the hangries (hunger-driven anger), and got back mental focus, energy, and a happy digestive tract. I have friends that have used a keto eating plan to lose 24–50 pounds in four months. My life partner Alan and my parents reduced their blood sugar levels. And I myself lost weight, even though that was not my intent.

For me, keto is so delicious. I love the cream sauces, avo slices, sour cream and guacamole, cheese on my taco salad, creamy dipping sauce for my veggies, salmon lox with cream cheese and capers, and the delicious taste of grass-fed/pastured meats as well as eating foods close to their natural state. So I will prefer farmers markets over conventional grocery stores and use small startup companies for my convenience foods.

But if I can't get it done that week because I'm busy or traveling, then I just hit my bare minimum of not exceeding my carb budget. This approach acknowledges that sometimes life doesn't go perfectly, and you can still stay on track.

2. The benefits of a moderate approach

There are so many books out there that can tell you the advantages of keto, or how to do it perfectly, or what to watch out for. I am not that person. I am the person that wants to help you do "good enough," sensible, effective keto because for me that is what has made it doable for so many years.

The first benefit of a moderate approach is that I find it easier to stick to my plan. I admire Olympic athletes, who often must execute perfectly on the day of competition. It doesn't matter how many other times they did their event perfectly, it only matters on that day that they are being measured. By not expecting myself to be perfect on keto, I find the strength to keep making keto-ish choices often enough that I find myself sticking to keto in a continuous fashion. Like a good sales indicator, my choices are good enough most the time to drive the overall trend of "up and to the right."

The second benefit of a moderate approach is that I'm more likely to stay with it for a long period of time. I have heard people say, "Oh, I did keto for a month but it didn't work for me" or that they had benefits but "fell off the wagon." The health benefits of a keto lifestyle need time to play out, and the best way to find out what you'll get out of this eating style is to do it consistently for a material amount of time. Give it at least two months, ideally six, so that you know you gave it a good go.

Most of all, be true to you. Everyone has an opinion they want to share with you, but only you know what is right for you. I'm counting on you to be reasonable. You need to run your plan past doctors you trust, as I'm neither a doctor nor a nutritionist. I'm just a gal who wants to share her food ideas and coping strategies with you.

The point of this book is to teach you enough tricks that eating low carb becomes an easy way of life. It's not sustainable to feel like you have to look up everything you eat, buy only the perfect right things, and cook every single meal. It's also not sustainable if you are not happy or if you cheat so much that you go in and out of keto. So let's get to the biggest joy stealer, and that is . . .

3. FOMO: fear of missing out

The reason I never liked diets or eating plans is that I didn't want to miss out on the things I love. I also didn't want to be separate from friends, like at a party or a family gathering where the whole point of the party is the food. I also didn't like a plan that didn't support having wine. C'mon, I have teenagers. Wine happens.

What are you most worried about missing out on while low-carbing?

- Bread
- Pasta
- Rice
- Baked Goodies (cakes, cookies, cobblers)
- Candy and Chocolate
- Crunchy/Salty
- Taco Night
- PIZZA

If you have FOMO about food, then I cannot imagine a better plan than a keto plan. In four years I have tackled quite a range of cravings I've had, and I will happily share everything I've learned with all of you. Brownies? Check! Pizza, tacos, and lasagna? Check, check, check!

With few exceptions, most anything you are craving is tied to a craving that is solvable.

Here is what I mean.

I love french fries and tater tots, which is funny because it's such a little kid food. If I out-and-out try to make keto french fries or tater tots, trust me, I have yet to find a truly equivalent counterpart. So I dug deeper. What was I really craving? Turns out I was craving the sensation of a hot, crunchy, salty, greasy moment dipped in ketchup and mayo. I know, I know, I've lost some of you at this point, but I'll get you in the next example, trust me.

Once I realized that I was actually craving crunchy/salty, then I just needed to solve for that. And it turns out that a lot of things fry up nicely with salt and can be dipped in mayo and low-carb ketchup. For example, many vegetables, once cut, diced, and mixed with something to hold them together, fry up nicely into a creative take on a tater tot or french fry. Veggie fritters can be quite satisfying! My point is this: think about taste, salty vs. sweet, texture, and mouthfeel, and usually a delicious keto counterpart can be arranged.

For my chocolate sweet fans, here is your example. I love classic chocolate cake with chocolate buttercream frosting, especially when cupcake-shaped. I used to have to make this from scratch with almond flour and such, but now you can buy boxed cake mixes that are low carb, add low-carb chocolate or white chocolate chips, even add low-carb caramels if you like, and frost that puppy with the most decadent cream cheese or chocolate buttercream, or even a nut-crusted German chocolate cake-type frosting, and no one will be the wiser. I know because I bring them to parties all the time, and they are very popular.

For my bread fans, here is a story for you. Bread is complex in that some people crave it because they actually just want to make avocado toast. Or a sandwich, or a crunchy grilled cheese. I have solutions for all of that. But there is also the sensory goodness of that crusty Italian bread dipped in olive oil. The straight up texture of bread is almost impossible to match in a low-carb diet. Does this mean you can't ever have artisanal bread again? The answer is not now. The answer is eventually, yes. The answer is bless your life in the short term, and you can return to it later. And until then, try a keto bread or a chaffle!

Also, let's talk alcohol.

Are you worried about having to give up your cocktail hour or your wine with dinner? The trick is, you can have wine with dinner, but then you must reduce the carbs in your day to account for it. When we want to relax and have a nice dinner evening together, my partner Alan and I usually make our first round a zero-carb cocktail and then have a glass of wine with dinner that matches the food. Your mileage may vary, and of course if you don't drink at all, that is the easiest of all carb allowances. Most wine is between 3–5 g a glass, so be judicious and you won't have to miss out.

And lastly, for my savory comfort food fans, I have mastered stews, curries, shepherd's pie, tacos, pizza, lasagna, gnocchi with vodka cream sauce, biscuits and gravy, and so much more. So when cravings hit, ask yourself what you really are needing, and honor it with some time to make exactly what you are craving and get it behind you.

And notice most of all that on a keto plan, you most likely can have the thing you want. Name a plan that allows pizza and tacos, let's be real.

When I was going through chemotherapy, one of the side effects was that I lost my sense of taste. For almost a year nothing tasted right, not even water, because literally everything tasted like nothing or some strange variant of mineral. All that was left was the texture of the food, and come to find out, texture alone can be a deal breaker.

I specifically remember trying a piece of cornbread, which I normally love. Instead, without the sensation of corn or sugar, it truly tasted like sand and paste. I couldn't even swallow it!

The worst part was that I still craved things, but nothing I ate could possibly meet the craving. If I was craving chocolate, nothing tasted like chocolate, including chocolate itself. I started to get pretty crabby because I couldn't have what I wanted.

The same is true for your low-carb journey. One of the best ways to make this journey joyful is to honor and figure out how to meet your cravings. If you are craving something crunchy and salty, then you need to fry up something and salt it. If you are craving chocolate, eat low-carb chocolate or melt some raw cacao with either coconut butter or heavy cream to make a drinking cocoa.

One of the biggies for me turned out to be pasta. I missed not only the straight up spaghetti and meatballs kind, but also the "foo-foo" cream sauce ones like pesto tortellini and beef stroganoff.

It turns out it's easier than you think to solve the pasta crisis.

When I first tried zoodles and vegetable substitutes like spaghetti squash, needless to say I didn't like them as much as pasta. I wanted that mouthfeel.

For me, the trick to handling cravings turned out to be giving thought to what I was wanting and finding an acceptable substitute. Zoodles would never be pasta for me, but when I made the sauce richer and added in more fats, the dish tasted so good it met the mark.

Here is an example: pretend I'm craving pasta carbonara. Creamy, a smidge bacony, and honestly a hassle to make at home because of the egg at the end.

I steamed the spaghetti squash and scooped it into a fry pan to dry out a bit. In a different pan I started with shallots and diced bacon, once browned I added bone broth and crème fraiche, by then the spaghetti squash had warmed, and I plated it with Romano cheese melting on top, then added the reduced creamy bacony sauce.

I wanted the creamy and bacony, so found a way to make the lean veggie noodles richer by compensating with the cheese and the sauce.

Therefore, let cravings be what they are, and then they lose their power. By acknowledging what you want and finding a solution, it loses its mystique of being a forbidden item and is relegated to the state of "thing you solved."

The nice thing about adhering to keto is that you lose your appetite in a good way. You can conquer the idea of having willpower because you simply are rarely hungry.

I am loving being the kind of person that doesn't need to eat that often. I love rarely feeling hungry. People say, "Wow, you have such great willpower!" Well, it's not willpower, it just "is." You know how after you've eaten a big meal, like Thanksgiving dinner, or whatever a big eating special occasion is in your culture? At that moment of feeling full, if someone offers you something yummy and you are already super full, do you really want it? Of course not.

Willpower to stick with this will get easier the longer you do it. The longer you do it, the less hungry you feel. When you are hungry for something, honor it by thinking through what you want and finding a keto alternative. And honestly, if you've been keto a while you usually can just have the thing you are seeking because one meal doesn't take you off track. That's the pot of gold at the end of the rainbow.

To find a keto alternative and to have what you want, you just need to be willing to put a little time into it until the marketplace demand can support more companies providing keto options. We haven't quite yet gotten to convenience keto. But we are getting there, and the more you vote with your dollar by supporting these new companies, the more they can flourish and make keto even easier than it is today.

For example, I used to have to make vanilla Häagen-Dazs ice cream from scratch. Now, you can get chocolate, nut-covered novelty ice cream bars from Enlightened Foods, and you can get premium creamy ice cream pints from Real Good Foods. At the end of the book, I have a way for you to get my current shopping list of amazing keto foods. Thankfully, the rate of change is encouraging, and I point you to a link because it changes by the month.

In the short term, you may need to make it from scratch. In the medium term, you may find a company making a product that matches what you are craving. Long term, you will be able to buy whatever you need whenever you need it.

Embrace your FOMO and your cravings and run right toward them with a delicious alternative. Far better to scratch the itch and get it over with, without sacrificing your goals.

4. How to deal with naysayers

Let's talk about naysayers.

When I first decided I didn't want to eat glucose anymore, after that day when I lay waiting for my PET scan, I started talking to others about how I wasn't going to eat carbs anymore. I was sure it was right for me, and I was so excited to talk about everything I was learning.

Well, you would have thought I was pronouncing that ALL carbs will no longer be available to ANYONE on planet Earth ANY more. I was amazed at how many people felt like they had to talk me out of it. It was like they were processing their own grief that they would feel if they were the ones giving up carbs. I heard a lot of fear-based things like:

"That's not safe you know, the body needs carbs."

"You're not going to do that to your kids are you? Kids need their carbs."

"I did that Atkins thing, all that bacon and grease, ugh!"

"All that fat is going to give you a heart attack!"

This could happen to you too, so here is my advice. Not everyone will want to share your enthusiasm for this liberating way of eating, and that's okay. In fact, watching you put as much dressing or sauce as you like on something you are eating probably makes some people a little jelly.

When we talk about how we eat, we invite people to share their opinions, good and bad. When we don't talk about how we eat, it's not so much on the table for discussion. I realized I was opening myself up for opinions or even unintentional criticism, and in the end I also realized that everyone gets to eat the way they want to without judgment. Also, I get to choose whether I filter their comments as criticism or not. I am not their opinions; I am the person listening to their opinions. In fact, I am also the person who can listen but not feel like I have to take on their opinions. They are just passing by.

In the end, I decided that what most people were doing was expressing how THEY would feel in my situation, and it's okay to have differing opinions, and most of all, I don't have to convince them that this is okay.

If naysayers try to fill your head with their concerns about how they feel about low-carbing, consider the approach of acknowledging their feelings without taking them on as your own, knowing that their opinions matter for them just like your opinions matter for you. You don't have to convince them you are right or they are wrong because only you know what is right for you, and you are not pronouncing anything regarding them. It is human nature to eek our stuff onto others, hoping they will make us feel okay, and the naysayer may be projecting their own feelings of grief or lack onto you.

The other way to deal with naysayers is to deeply know your personal WHY.

To have success with Sensible Keto, you need to have a sustainable WHY. If your first answer is something like "lose weight," consider asking yourself more follow-up questions like, "Why does losing weight matter?" or "What does a successful amount of weight loss look like?" If you keep questioning the answers you come up with, usually you will eventually arrive at the heart of the matter.

If asking yourself "Why?" is not meaningful for you, ask yourself what you were hoping would happen as a result of going keto. Hope is powerful and drives much of our decision-making.

In my case it was cancer survivorship, but for you it could be feeling confident enough in your own skin that you go after that promotion or new career you've been thinking about or take that courageous first step toward a different life than the one you're currently living.

My "why" is not even based in known fact.

In my twenties, I used to do metric century bike rides with my friends. I was really into heart-healthy eating, which back then meant low fat. In my zeal to avoid fat, I ate highly processed alternatives like lower-fat margarines and high-fiber breads and pastas. It's funny how it somehow seemed better to eat what I now know to be a bad oil product.

It's also how I learned about the difference between burning sugar and burning fat. I remember being right about the forty-mile mark, and I was in a fog. I couldn't pedal anymore, my friends were way ahead of me, and I was lying on the side of the road, unable to really move, staring at an Oreo that had been smashed by several bikes and seriously considering eating it!

Thankfully, as I lay there, my body finally caught up to my fuel needs and made it into fat-burning mode. I sailed through the last part of the race drawing on the fat reserves of my body, and I vowed to do a better job to plan ahead to not "bonk" like that in the future. It was my first experience with the idea of burning fat for fuel.

I found out that if you restrict your carbs, and you are not a type 1 diabetic, then you can switch your body into more of a fat-burning mode. In a fat-burning mode, the "food" molecules for the body are ketones, and healthy cells can use those for fuel. Cancer cells theoretically cannot.

I love imagining cancer cells watching stuff go by in the bloodstream saying, "Darn, can't eat that, can't eat that either, can't eat that, hmm can't eat that either" and wondering if they will starve to death.

I didn't go looking for proof that this actually happens. I'm okay with just visualizing it, laughing about it, and continuing to eat this way. In the last four years, my cancer markers look good, I have plenty of energy, I'm no longer a slave to "must eat every two hours or else" low blood sugar mood swings, I rock a bikini in my fifties, I'm never hungry, and overall it's working for me.

It's working for other people too. There are accounts all over the web of people losing significant weight, reducing symptoms of autism and seizures, getting rid of migraines, reversing their A1C, and more.

More and more, keto is showing up in newsstands, on the covers of magazines, and on store shelves. I predict it's the next big trend in food categories, like paleo and gluten-free were previously.

A brief trip through Pinterest, Facebook, Instagram, Amazon Prime, and YouTube with search terms like keto, low-carb, LCHF (low-carb high-fat), ketogenic, and more show how prevalent keto is as a trending hashtag.

When reading the good and the bad, remember that Sensible Keto does not mean eat a ton of red meat and fatty foods. Sensible keto means make the best choices you can no matter where you are. When you are at home, eat well! Choose grass-fed and pastured meats in moderation, dark leafy green veggies, and quality fats like avocado. When you are traveling, eat conventional foods but still avoid carbs.

One of the top criticisms of eating keto is that it is not good long term. However, what these critics fail to realize is that it was never meant to be a forever strategy. It's a great way to start training your body to pull fuel in a different way and jump-start your health goals. It's motivating to "be on a diet" but eat satisfying foods and feel full. It can heal a broken relationship with food. It can give control over hunger so that better choices can creep in. It can confer metabolic flexibility over time. After this many years of my Sensible Keto approach, I can eat whatever I want whenever I want to, even over 50. This was not the case in my 30s and 40s.

My life partner Alan flies a lot for work, and he came home one day asking me if I'd seen *The Magic Pill* on Netflix. He was not low-carbing with me at the time, and he literally said, "I think you'll like it; it's like talking to you for 90 minutes."

I had not seen it, and in general I don't like to watch food documentaries because of their truth. I'm never going to be that person that gives up occasional fast food or does it right all the time. But I watched it and loved it and urge you to consider watching it too.

Some other resources that can help you feel better about eating more fat and less carbs are as follows:

- "The science of low carb and keto," by Dr. Andreas Eenfeldt, MD and Dr. Bret Scher, MD. https://www.dietdoctor.com. The Diet Doctor website is ad-free and funded by people, not product sales.
- "Effect of lower versus higher red meat intake on cardiometabolic and cancer outcomes," *Annals of Internal Medicine*, 2019. https://annals.org.
- "Long-term effects of a ketogenic diet in obese patients," *Experimental & Clinical Cardiology*. https://www.ncbi.nlm.nih.gov.
- The cookbook authors I recommend in Chapter 23

My hope is that by knowing your why, learning about other people's whys, and recognizing that others may be processing their own fears and FOMO when they naysay to you, you will emerge confident and victorious that you've got this. Because you do.

5. Get all the way into ketosis

Yesterday I had lunch with a friend who noticed I was eating just the middle of my sandwich and not eating the bread. He said, "I'm sorta low-carbing too, but I keep falling off the wagon." Think about what he just said. Some days he stays below his threshold, and some days he does not. That means he's making the effort to avoid carbs, which is a huge output of energy and effort, but because he never quite makes it through, he's never a fat burner and is always sacrificing.

It will take a few days, or maybe a week or two, but the most important first step is to make it all the way into a fat-burning state and STAY THERE. All the way! I'm moderate on all aspects of keto except this.

Think about it. Do you really want to do the work of learning a new way of eating and not get the benefits?

Loosely speaking, your body starts by burning carbs or fat, one or the other. In the beginning, as a carb burner, if you eat keto some days and not others and thus remain a carb burner and not a fat burner, then you are doing a LOT of work for LITTLE benefit. And you'd probably be gaining weight or increasing body inflammation. You'd definitely be feeding the cancer candidates.

And notice my verb choice above: I said sacrificing. When you play around with low-carbing and stay just on the fringe of being a fat burner, you don't have the benefits like feeling full and low appetite. Recall my Thanksgiving dinner example: if you've just finished a huge meal with pie and everything and are no longer hungry, wouldn't you have the willpower of a superhero?

I urge you to take the week and get all the way through.

It took me three tries to become a low-carber. I failed the first two times and gave up. I now know how to save you that agony of crossing over. And don't worry, the more you do this, the easier it gets.

The first time I tried it was in 2013, when low-carbing was less of a thing. For the first two weeks I ate only the recipes in the book I was reading, and they were not only low carb but also low fat. Imagine recipes like a bunch of cabbage and veggies in a soup and only eating soup and simple unseasoned proteins throughout the day. I was miserable. I had no energy, I was starving, I had a low-grade headache, and on top of it all I don't even think I ever crossed over to becoming a fat burner. I gave up. And I can tell you right now, it was because that eating plan did not have enough fat.

The second time I tried it was in 2014. The program I tried this time had step-by-step foods you ate at certain times on certain days. As I already mentioned, despite plenty of ability, I have not mastered putting my keys in the same place every time I enter the house. Imagine me on a plan with specific timings and intervals. I am not that organized!

At least this time, after four long days of not being able to get out of bed or focus, I came through and was a fat burner. I could see the benefit. But over time, I just couldn't put that much time into my eating plan. I don't remember how long this program lasted, but it was not a permanent change for me.

The last time I tried it was in 2015, and thank goodness I made it and have been eating this way ever since. For me, the trick was to indulge in good fats to make the transition more joyful feeling, such as ordering veggies with a velvety sauce, and for sure my focus was on what tastes good. I also for a few days didn't worry about salt intake and ate more than normal to make up for how much water I was processing. I also found that because of the wisdom gained from my two earlier attempts, I didn't have flu symptoms and crossed over in a day or two. The trick for me was more salt (or electrolytes) and more fat.

The advantage to getting all the way through and past the "flu" is to quickly get to the easier side of being keto. Being all the way in keto is useful as an appetite suppressant, so you can slow down and make better choices throughout the day.

Before I started low-carbing, I was a classic carb burner. By that I mean that if I didn't eat every 2–4 hours, I became irrational, had difficulty making decisions, and maybe wasn't so nice to be around. Given that time interval, it meant I had to eat frequently throughout the day, which if you think about it takes up a bunch of free time that can be spent doing other things.

The nice thing about being keto for a length of time is that I lost my "must eat every 2–4 hours or will kill people" and became very calm and patient about food. I am rarely hungry, which gives me plenty of time to pick and eat something that is appropriate for me. When I am in this state, I am not hungry, so it's no longer a matter of having willpower. So get yourself all the way in, and let the rest of the journey get easier. You deserve to have a peaceful relationship with food.

How to know if you are all the way into ketosis

The simplest way to know is by how you feel. If it follows many people's experience, then you will experience the symptoms of keto flu, especially the acetone taste on your breath, and then those symptoms will abate and be followed by an incredible feeling of energy and a noticeable drop in appetite. You may also begin to lose weight in places previously considered stubborn (like around your tummy).

If you are the kind of person who likes to know for sure, you can get strips from the drugstore that measure how many ketones are in your urine. I especially liked the product called Ketostix by Bayer (yep, just like the aspirin, same company). However, over time this measure is less accurate because you can be in ketosis without measurable ketone bodies being thrown off in your urine.

This can also be demoralizing if you are like my dear friend Jill, who kept measuring and thinking she had not made it, but it turned out her strips were weak and not measuring correctly. When she tried one of my strips she saw that she was measuring a deep purple (high ketones).

As a side note, the goal with these strips is not to stay always in the purple, because the strips are measuring ketones in the urine, which can vary throughout the day. Just measuring that ketones are present is a good sign, although how you feel is an even more important sign.

The most accurate way to measure is by measuring ketones in your blood. You can buy kits on Amazon from companies like Keto-Mojo. You buy test strips similar to diabetic test strips and test your blood at a similar time of day.

After years of measuring, I have to say I've become quite lazy about it and rarely do it. I can tell when I'm eating too many carbs because my body will change. I'll start to crave crazy things or feel "off." My hope is that over time, a Sensible Keto approach for you evolves into this intuitive-style approach where you have all the benefits you want without slavish attention to every detail.

How to reduce the symptoms of keto flu

The first time I journeyed toward a state of ketosis, it was like I got hit by a Mack truck. I couldn't get out of bed, and I'm never that way. I had horrible breath despite brushing my teeth a lot. It came up through my gut and was so embarrassing. I felt so unmotivated, had a headache, and my gut was complaining.

For four days, I struggled to make it through each day without crying or lashing out. I thought I was going to starve to death. I was not sure I was going to make it.

Then on the fifth day, the clouds parted, the angels sang, and I wanted to run a marathon. By the way, I am not a runner.

What I've since learned is that I was not eating enough fat, nor was I managing my electrolyte balance. I was peeing a lot and not replacing the salt, magnesium, and potassium, so I was mildly dehydrated and not eating enough.

To reduce the symptoms of transitioning from carb burner to fat burner, take in extra salt, take magnesium and potassium supplements, and be hypervigilant about consuming enough fat per day, even if it's not a good fat. It's just for a few days, and it's better to keep yourself moving forward to fat burner than it is to do it perfectly.

When I was in induction, I kept it simple. I ate eggs, avocado, meats, butter, cheese, coffee with heavy cream, salads with olive oil or a delicious creamy dressing, and my personal favorite, oven bacon. My goal was to add fats to a meal to ensure I was full. When crossing over to keto is the goal, then let the higher-arching goals slip for a few days to get to the other side. There is plenty of time to be less bad and more organic. At first I focused on just getting through.

My approach was to eat until I was full so that I didn't feel deprived, eat more fat to ease my headaches, and add in potassium, magnesium, and salt to make up for electrolyte loss. I even added in Smartwater (an electrolyte water).

Here is how it plays out in real life.

For breakfast, if I was making eggs, I'd also add avocado or low-carb sautéed veggies and make a big bowl. If you start with a good fat, high heat, toss in the veggies, don't stir much, and use a high-sided pan, you can make this dish in a few minutes. I'd also toss in a premade Alfredo or make a scratch cream sauce, depending on how much time I had. The point is, I ate a lot so I didn't feel deprived, I ate the right things to keep my carb count low, I added fats to feel happy about this change, and I added salt and minerals to maintain my electrolyte balance.

There are many great experts out there that have already covered how to make it through induction, so all I will add is that for me, I just kept it simple and ate extra healthy fats and drank a lot of water to keep the dreaded keto breath at bay. More fat, more water, and staying below 20 grams of net carbs a day is what worked for me and my friends.

6. How to keep track while eating keto

With Sensible Keto, I recommend that you watch just two things: number of net grams of carbs per day and number of grams of protein per day. For the latter, you can use a protein calculator. This is to help ensure that you get into nutritional ketosis and stay there.

By watching only two measures, it's easier to focus, and it won't hurt you in the long run. Of course, watching every macro and everything is a more complete method. But if by watching everything you get overwhelmed and give up, then that is not very sensible now, is it?

I also urge you to let go of the scale for a while. As you shift from carb burner to fat burner, you may slim up while gaining pounds due to muscle mass. It's better to measure less and check in with yourself more. Ask yourself how you feel, and let the drape of your clothes help you see that things are getting better.

So back to food intake measures. Start by knowing your carb budget and protein budget expressed in net grams. Why these two macros?

Excess protein is treated like carbs, so google a protein calculator and enter your weight, age, and activity level to figure out how many grams of protein per day to eat.

Notice I didn't say count calories. Wait, what?

That's right. In the beginning, I don't believe in counting calories unless you are not getting results and you are in a review of everything you are eating, which means that for a week or two you are counting literally everything to figure out what's not working for you. For most people, limiting carbs is a sufficient place to start and keeps the focus where it belongs until you get the hang of keto.

I also didn't say to count grams of fat. If you are worried about how much fat you eat, and I'm talking about quality fats like avocado, tree nuts, fish, and grass-fed/pastured meats, then ask yourself why.

As a populace, we fear fat because the cereal industry giants have programmed us so well since the introduction of processed convenience foods in the fifties that we can't believe fat is okay. As I mentioned, watch *The Magic Pill* on Netflix. It's the fastest way to catch up on why we as a public still believe that fat is the enemy. I also recommend reading anything by Dr. David Perlmutter.

Lastly, I suggest starting with counting net carbs rather than total carbs. The net carbs is equal to total carbs minus fiber grams and minus my approved list of sugar substitute grams (for example, Allulose and Erythritol). Purists will disagree, and that is okay.

Sensible Keto is about keeping it easy, and part of keeping it easy is that you don't need to change anything unless you are in a review of why you are not getting results. Therefore, unless you are troubleshooting, start your journey by just counting the net carbs and protein in your daily budget to keep it easy and manageable.

You may be wondering how to count carbs in the beginning, so let's make it easy. I used an app called Carb Manager, which I like because it lists the values for both raw foods and store-bought prepared foods. You can even scan the bar codes of things to get their carb count. And you can enter recipes you develop on your own as foods so that future logging is easier.

When I first started low-carbing, I swear I was checking the app a million times a day. The nice thing about that constant feedback is that I started to naturally learn the carb counts of various foods. Now, I don't look at anything, I just intuitively eat. After four years, I promise you too will know what you choose to eat without thinking about it.

Notice I didn't say what you can and cannot eat. You are not a little kid waiting for permission, you are a beautiful adult who wants to be healthier. When we use verbs like *can* or *let*, we are giving away our power to others. We feel like we are the victim. When we use words like *choose* or *will*, we stay in control, and we are the ones making the decisions and taking action.

Consider these phrases. Which person seems more in control of their joy and their life?

I should have called the dentist, but other things took priority.	I could have called the dentist, but I chose to work on high-er-priority items.
Thanks for letting me spend time with you today.	Thanks for spending time with me today.
I can't eat that, it's not low carb.	I choose not to eat that, it's not low carb.
I have to go pick up the kids.	I get to go pick up the kids.
I'll try to get back to you later.	I will get back to you later.

This journey is a journey you are choosing to take because you want to. If it's not, I urge you to ask yourself why you are on this journey. Be purposeful in your intentions, so that on days that everything is coming at you, you maintain a strong stance. This is true in eating keto, and it's true in living a magnificent life. Stay in your personal power because only you know what is right for you. You don't need to fritter away your power on convincing others.

Use a protein calculator

One of the reasons I sometimes shy away from using the word "keto" is that for some people the word keto means a ton of meat. Recalling the old Atkins days, keto to some means bacon and meat and being a total carnivore. In fact, a common thing I hear is that people feel that protein is a safe item and therefore, the more the merrier on keto.

That is not my experience.

Excess protein is treated like carbs in the body, so if you are not having results, the first place I'd look is at grams of protein per day. The optimal amount of protein per day varies by person and is a function of age, activity level, weight, and other things.

I mentioned before to use a calculator that takes into account your age, weight, and activity level. A good online calculator can be found on my website, ketokimber.com

Or, if you want to calculate it manually, just multiply your weight by 0.36, factoring a bit up or down if you are trying to gain muscle or lose weight. That number in grams is how much protein to shoot for each day.

The value of carb-counting apps

At first, it may seem overwhelming to keep track of how much a given food item is worth in grams of carbs. The way I started was to look everything up in an app called Carb Manager before I ate it, which over time taught me the carb values of most foods.

The good thing about using any of the carb-tracking apps is that you not only improve your chance of success by keeping a good count of your daily intake, but you also teach yourself what is high and low carb so that you learn to create your meals for the day without looking.

I used to track everything, and I needed to do so because I didn't know how much different foods would "cost" me, and I wasn't having results because there were many sneaky hidden sources of carbs that I was not accounting for.

Now I don't track at all and still stay keto because I generally know the values of the foods I eat.

You may wonder why a book about sensible and easy keto would coach people to count everything. There is a simple answer. Although I want to make keto as easy as possible for you, I also want you to have success. When people are not having success with keto, upon discussion we always find a hidden source of carbs that they were not counting that took them over their budget.

In the same way that good goals are SMART (specific, measurable, attainable, relevant, and time-based), Sensible Keto is also SMART. We can be loose about a lot of things, but to have success being a low-carber, be sure to be smart and quantifiable in your approach.

7. Strive for nutritional diversity

Let's talk diversity for a sec. Diversity is great in workplaces, but it's great in eating plans too. For example, if you just get all your protein from beef, you are missing out on the side benefits of other proteins.

Gut check. Which inherently seems better for you?

- A. Your daily protein comes from just a hamburger and some taco meat.
- B. Your daily protein comes from a little bit of each of these: meat, veggies, and pastured dairy.

Ideally, you eat a wide variety of foods each day, so that all the little extra things that come with your protein source add up to a well-rounded multivitamin effect.

I'm always happy to add protein from veggies when I can, and we will talk in a sec how to make that yummy because as you know, I don't live life to settle for non-yummy.

Let's take kale as an example.

Kale?

Yes, kale. And if you are saying you don't like kale, I urge you to at least hear me out.

I don't like kale when it has these huge stems, it's in huge hunks you can barely chew, and while eating it you feel like you are chewing wood.

I get it.

The trick to eating vegetables is usually the size of the bite, the tenderness of the bite, and the taste of it. If the kale was de-stemmed, shredded into small ribbons, and mixed in with your Chinese chicken salad, would you perhaps dislike it a little less? Or (kids, cover your ears) what if I blended it into a brownie and you didn't know it was there, would you still say you don't like kale? What if it was sautéed into a tender bite draped in your favorite sauce?

Kale is worth embracing. It is a nutrient-dense dark leafy green, and we know from childhood that those are good. They are not only a protein source but also a source of that hard-to-get vitamin K, as well as vitamins A and C. Add in calcium, potassium, and a smidge of omega-3 fatty acids, and you have to admit it is an efficient little nutritional package. One cup of kale has two grams of protein.

I mean, c'mon, doesn't that sound worth embracing? Worth fitting in? And if not kale, how about other little superfood veggies?

It turns out that many veggies are that way and also, sometimes surprisingly, fresh herbs. I keep a small flat pot by my kitchen sink with basil, parsley, cilantro, mint, and other herbs because they are relatively hard to kill if you at least do dishes a few times a week. It's an easy matter to watch their water level when you (hopefully) are at the sink now and again.

No window by your kitchen sink? No window at all? How about the bathroom, and you could check it when you brush your teeth?

If you are just sure you can't grow herbs anywhere inside or outside your home, then make friends with a gardening neighbor or buy them in the veggie section of your store.

Lately, I have been enjoying microgreens as a way to add more green nutrients to my diet. Microgreens are the older siblings of sprouts. When I was a kid in the 70s, I remember my mom going on an alfalfa sprout kick, and I never really liked them and have avoided them my whole adult life.

However, as I ate out in fine restaurants, I started to see microgreens, which taste a lot better to me. Microgreens are the young seedling versions of leafy greens and vegetables, and they are a few days older than sprouts.

For example, sprouts are seedlings 2–4 days old, whereas microgreens are seedlings 7–10 days old. Studies have shown that vegetables like broccoli and kale are more nutritious at 7–10 days old than they are as full-grown plants, and they take far less land and water than their conventionally grown counterparts.[1]

Best of all, they grow easily at home on your kitchen counter within a week. I am a huge fan of local Sacramento startup Hamama for creating kits that you water once, use your home's ambient light, and are

---

[1] Xiao, Z. et al. (2012). Assessment of Vitamin and Carotenoid Concentrations of Emerging Food Products: Edible Microgreens. *Journal of Agricultural and Food Chemistry, 60 (31)*, 7565–7768. https://pubs.acs.org/doi/full/10.1021/jf300459b

guaranteed to grow. Because microgreens sit on the counter and are ready each week, they are fresher than what you find at the store, and it's easy to toss them on top of any meal as an added nutritional punch.

Another way to add diversity is to add fresh herbs to your diet such as leafy basil, parsley, and cilantro. Similar to dark leafy greens like spinach, fresh herbs can add vitamins A, C, and K as well as antioxidants to your diet and in some cases even provide an anti-inflammatory effect. In the same way an Italian caprese salad is full of fresh basil leaves, almost any dish benefits from a handful of diced fresh herbs for flavor and added nutrition.

As you make choices throughout your day of what to eat, consider adding more veggies, microgreens, and herbs to your diet to give yourself a diverse set of nutritional benefits and keep your interest up, too!

8. How to do modified keto when the rest of the family won't

When I started to eat this way, my family was not super excited. My kids like what they like, and who could blame them for not wanting to eat the way I eat? Alan was also not interested in eating low carb, and since I am the cook in this family, at first I was making two meals twice a day to accommodate my family and me.

It didn't take me long to get smart about this. Most everything my family likes to eat has carbs in it, but there is usually something about it that can be modified to accommodate a low-carber. For example, if the family wants spaghetti, then I make one sauce for all of us using pastured meat and a healthful jarred marinara, but for me I make a substitute for the pasta.

Or if it's taco night, many, many aspects of a taco bar are low carb, and it's the taco shells or the tortillas and chips that are not low carb. I make the taco meat and the fixings for everyone, and then I either substitute low-carb tortillas (store-bought, or when I have time, handmade), or I just make a pile of taco salad and call it good. The best part for me is the sour cream and guacamole, and smashed avocado is thankfully very keto-friendly.

If we are BBQing that night, I make the meat for all of us, minus any sugary marinades, then make sides for all and make sure that one of them is veggies or something I can eat. There are so ways to prep meat to be delicious for all without adding sugar, such as using Worcestershire sauce, soy sauce, coconut aminos, sesame oil, seasoned salts, etc. I have since found low-carb BBQ sauces that are quite good, plus I can make my own using low-carb ketchup, allulose or other low-carb sugars, and seasonings.

I could go on with more and more examples, but the point is to simply evaluate what you are making for the family and then make it most of the way until you have to deviate to make your part low carb.

I leave both the low carb and the regular carb items out for all, and over time my family is joining in on some of my keto alternatives. Alan loved the taste of my zucchini-based tortilla substitutes and now prefers them to regular tortillas. You may find that as you keep setting an example and keep exhibiting better health outcomes while eating keto, more and more of your friends and family will join in.

SETUP FOR SUCCESS

> Pro tip: Organize close to point of use: put spices and umami and fats near the stove, put mug cakes and sugars together, buy mixes and pair with delish add-ins like white chocolate chips.

There has never been a better time to try this way of eating. I used to have to mail order everything and spend a lot of time on weekends making stuff from scratch. Thankfully, now there is a nice blend of good companies you can support by buying from them online, as well as cooking a bit yourself and even heating stuff up from the freezer from brands now being carried in most major grocery stores.

To make low-carbing easy, I am prepared with common low-carb substitutes for things I need to bake or cook with like sugar, healthier fats, flour substitutes, proteins, and seasonings. When I come home from a business trip and haven't had time to shop, it helps to have some items I can whip together so I don't go off the ranch.

For example, from my pantry, without having gone to a store first, I can open a can of chicken, mix with mayo, pickles, and water chestnuts, and wrap it in a low-carb tortilla from the freezer. Voila, last minute chicken salad. Bonus if I find some still-okay cabbage in the bottom of the fridge.

Or, I can heat up something I made from another night that is waiting in the freezer because I always make more than I need to build up my stockpile. When I cook a meal, I make double or triple so I can store some of it before serving.

Another idea is to brown beef or vegan meat crumbles in a pan, microwave a 10 oz bag of frozen riced cauliflower while it's browning, puree the cauli in the Cuisinart or a bullet blender with your desired fats and salt (for example grass-fed butter, cream cheese, cheddar cheese, cashew "cream" cheese), and layer the two together for a simple shepherd's pie.

Part of making it easy is to not run out of options. When I'm hungry without options I make bad decisions!

By the way, when you make a double or triple batch of something, put aside a few freezer meals for yourself before serving your family. If you pull it out first, they won't miss it, especially because you've made double or triple what you normally make. If you wait and do it after dinner, somehow there is not always enough to put up for later.

9. What to have on hand

To get started, there are a few things you will want to purchase to make keto easier. The first thing I'm usually asked about is sugar substitutes, and I have a very sensitive tummy so for me it's these sugar alternatives in order of preference: allulose, monk fruit, stevia, yacon syrup, inulin, erythritol, and xylitol.

My dirty list that I would never, ever consider eating because they make me ill are sucralose, maltitol, and aspartame.

We will talk more about sugar substitutes in a minute, but for now this is my bare minimum list of things needed in the first week to have success getting into ketosis:

- Eggs
- Butter
- Heavy cream
- Uncured quality bacon, or if you don't like bacon, then choose turkey bacon or your favorite breakfast meat
- A few heads of romaine or a box of mixed salad greens
- A bag of granulated Lakanto Monkfruit or Swerve erythritol blend (if you need sugar in your coffee or for other immediate sugar needs)
- A bag of spinach, some kale, a head of broccoli, or some dark green low-carb veggie you could enjoy in scrambled eggs or as a side dish
- A rotisserie chicken from Costco or your grocery store
- A package of Mission brand low-carb tortillas
- Ideally, a hunk of cheese that you box grate or run through your Cuisinart, because block cheese is lower-carb than prepackaged shredded cheese. If not, then a bag of shredded cheese (don't let details prevent a win).
- A pound or so of ground beef (ideally grass fed, but again don't overthink things in the beginning). If I'm buying conventional ground beef I choose 80% meat, 20% fat because it has a nice loose feel in the pan and creates a tastier outcome.
- Some bulk pork sausage, Italian if you have a seasoning choice, to create spaghetti Bolognese-style.
- A jar of marinara. I shop the aisle looking for the best carb value.
- A spaghetti squash
- Avocadoes if you like them
- Sour cream

With this list, you can make stir fry, omelets, tacos, spaghetti, quesadillas, sandwich wraps, and more. It will be enough to get you through induction, which for many is the hardest part. If you are a coffee drinker, add the heavy cream to help with fat consumption.

While trying to cross over, please avoid wine and do not even consider drinking beer. If this is a showstopper, then switch to hard alcohol in soda water, Bai or Core fruit drinks for low-carb cocktails, and for beer switch to either Lagunitas DayTime, Corona Premier, or Michelob Ultra to keep carb counts below 20, including food intake for the day.

Sugar substitutes

So back to what to keep around, and since this is the first thing I always get asked about, let's start with sugar substitutes.

Why do you need sugar alternatives on a low-carb diet?

Well, because sweets signal to us that we've had dessert and we are all done eating. Also, by having a sugar substitute we can sweeten things if needed like coffee, tea, low-carb cocktails, and baked goods and can even sweeten half and half and freeze it, which with vanilla or raw cacao makes an excellent substitute keto ice cream.

I am a fan of allulose, erythritol, stevia, monk fruit, and inulin. I'm somewhat of a fan of xylitol, but because it's toxic to dogs I don't keep it in my house. I am absolutely not a fan of maltitol, sucralose, aspartame, and other sweeteners found in mainstream grocery store brands because they give me a tummy ache. My understanding is that these digest too early in the intestines, which is what causes issues.

So let's cover each of my favorites:

Allulose is a new entrant I learned about from Sweet Logic that crisps up in baked goods like real sugar. It does not have the cool aftertaste that some of the others have and can trick even the most discerning non-low-carbers. Although you can buy mug cakes and cake mixes from Sweet Logic with allulose in them already, you also can just buy the allulose straight up for your own baking.

Erythritol is made from fermented apples and can be found almost everywhere under the brand name Swerve. It also can be bought on Amazon under a wealth of names. What I like about Swerve is that it comes in many forms, such as brown, granular, and powdered (cream cheese frosting, anyone?) as well as in cake and cookie mixes. It has a slightly cool aftertaste, but it is very slight. When I make snowball cookies that is actually a desirable trait!

Monk fruit is exciting because it's literally a fruit, so I feel good about it. It is also pretty easy to find both in mainstream grocery stores and online. I'm also happy to watch the growth of Lakanto, a brand that not only makes the brown and regular sugar, but also maple syrup, pancake mix, cake mixes, and more. This brand is introducing new products all the time and is relatively easy to find both in regular grocery stores and online.

Stevia is both a plant and a very sweet-tasting sugar substitute. It can taste bitter but blends nicely with erythritol. It's in little packets at places like Starbucks, so you can have your sweet coffee without adding carbs.

When I'm baking totally from scratch, I often mix the sugars together to get a blended and pleasing taste. For example, in my recipes section I have a cheesecake that uses granular allulose for the crust, finely ground monk fruit for the cheesecake part, and powdered sugar Swerve (erythritol) for the sour cream topping. You could just use Swerve for the whole thing—since cheesecake is cold a cooling effect is not really a problem, but blending definitely takes it up a notch.

When I first started on this journey, I needed to buy the good sugar substitutes online, but as the years go on and "keto" is becoming a big thing, I can find brands I trust in major chain grocery stores and health food stores. I am a big believer in letting my shopping dollars inform the market, so I love supporting the startups that are entering this food category and having to compete against larger, more established food manufacturers.

For example, let's talk straight up candy. When I first heard of Curly Girlz and Paula Trenda, she and her daughter had a handmade chocolate shop in MN that made both keto and conventional candies. Now, they are so wildly popular that they only make low-carb candies. This holiday season I bought chocolate covered sea salt caramels, homemade fudge, and truffles, all made with the ingredients I trust. And how great did it feel to support a mom-and-daughter-owned company?! Yeah, it felt like the right thing to do.

To get a list of all my favorite staples, like which brown sugar versus which powdered sugar, which baking mix, etc., go to ketokimber.com and download my latest cheat sheet. I update it constantly with my product reviews and new product finds.

Healthy fats

My method for feeling full is to be sure to add healthy fats everywhere I can in the form of sauces, frying, and hidden ingredients. An example of what I mean by hidden ingredients is as follows.

When I fry up eggs for breakfast, I am heavy-handed with the ghee or Kerrygold pastured butter. Or when I brown grass-fed ground beef for taco night, I usually add a tablespoon of duck fat, which no one sees but everyone loves the taste of. It's hidden but universally beloved.

I also like to add fat to salads, because on their own they sometimes don't fill me up. Instead of oil and vinegar, how about Green goddess, ranch, blue cheese, creamy cilantro, or anything else that appeals that is creamy? If you don't like dairy, you can still make a creamy dressing from mashed avocado, miso, crushed nuts, and dairy substitutes like almond, coconut, or cashew milk.

In the spirit of keeping it easy, I buy EPIC duck fat by the jar and freeze 1 TB doses in an ice cube tray or silicone mini muffin pan. Once frozen, I pop them into a Ziploc that lives in my freezer door for a quick addition to sauces or dishes that need a little umami.

I also keep sour cream in the fridge because it lasts a long time, and you can deglaze a pan, add your favorite stock, reduce down, and at the end stir in the sour cream for a quick pan sauce.

By adding avocado, duck fat, butter, ghee, or avocado oil to things, I up the satisfaction level and feel full faster.

Let's tackle another fat I love: cheese and dairy.

Audible gasp! It's inflammatory! It's not good for you! It's true, some people cannot have dairy, and thankfully there are now so many nut and other milk alternatives like Cultured Kitchen and Kite Hill that I trust if you are one of those people, you already know what to do.

But for the rest of you pizza-loving folk, let's talk cheese and dairy. Get the best dairy you can afford, and don't be afraid to try sheep and goat cheese. At Trader Joe's and better grocery stores, I've found goat and sheep versions of cheddar, mozzarella, and more that are delicious.

And let's be real, if the alternative is that you were eating fast food or pizza anyway, is it so crazy to add in some interest to every meal in the form of cheese or a creamy salad dressing or a zesty sauce? I found out that I have a fat tooth more than a sweet tooth, so I get pretty excited about anything in a good sauce.

On Christmas Day, my best friend and stepdaughter Ashley made seared asparagus that had crispy tips, served with a lemony tarragon cream sauce that I cannot wait to try to make myself. Imagine the crispy bite of veggie paired with a bright lemony sauce made from mayo and olive oil, a ton of fresh lemons, and the tarragon. For me, that was way better than dessert. And it was totally low carb despite its decadent taste.

Just eating asparagus would have left me hungry. But paired with the sauce, it was a delightful and satisfying addition to our brunch menu.

The way she made it was to start with heavy cream and mayo in a saucepan, add an amazing amount of lemon, and temper it with the tarragon. By tasting it as she went, it came out amazing, and against the background of the crispy asparagus tips it was mind-blowing.

I also like to buy crème fraiche, or if you cannot find that, buy sour cream. Crème fraiche is sold in tubs like sour cream and can be found at better grocery stores. Imagine you've just browned meat or mushrooms and are now making a gravy. I start by adding bone broth to get the bits up, add in some arrowroot dissolved in water (a lower-carb substitute for thickening agents like flour or cornstarch), reduce it down until it tastes savory (adjusting with salt, pepper, Worcestershire sauce, onions, or garlic), and then as a finishing touch bring down the heat and stir in the cream.

Instant cream sauce, good on top of the meat or mushrooms you just browned. If you don't like cow dairy, there are goat and sheep alternatives, and even vegetarian companies like Kite Hill make cream cheese and sour cream-type alternatives.

So my hot tip is to watch for ways to add fat to your meals in the form of hidden fats, dressings, sauces, and cheese. Good fats are your friend and will help up the joy factor with food.

10. Baking

Almond flour is available everywhere these days, and you can even find it in different levels of grind, from coarse to very fine. Since it makes a wetter dough, it's good to mix in a tablespoon of coconut flour, which is incredibly dry.

Some recipes you will find call for an ingredient I had never heard of until low-carbing: psyllium husk, which I buy in bulk on Amazon or from my local health food store. If you like hearty wheat bread texture, adding psyllium husk not only adds a nice texture, it also ups the fiber, which positively affects the net carbs.

When I first started on this journey, I would look for ways to modify a conventional flour recipe to be low carb by switching in the almond flour and substituting out the sugar for one of my favorite alternatives. However, since baking is often like a science experiment with specific chemistry, the results were not what I was hoping for.

What ended up working for me was to follow other bloggers' recipes until I started to get the hang of low-carb baking on my own. Another option is to start with an existing cake or brownie mix and uplevel it from there.

For example, I use the Swerve vanilla cake mix and add in pecans, brown sugar, and rum to make a rum cake. Or, I use Diabetic Kitchen's brownie mix and add in white chocolate chips from Lily's. In my shopping list at the end of this book, I list all the brands I've been successful with so you can find them too. And I'll give you the recipe for the rum cake! My list is always evolving as new entrants hit the market, so visit my blog at withpurejoy.com for the latest.

II. Frying

When I say fryer, are you thinking about the greasy baskets at a diner? I am not talking about frying in oils that turn bad as soon as you heat them, nor am I talking about frying up carbs. Because I live near a Costco, I just use avocado oil for everything because I can buy a large amount, it tastes like nothing, and will take on other good flavors I'm adding like duck fat or butter.

I grew up loving french fries. I love salty crunchy. If you like salty crunchy too, I recommend frying things as a way to enjoy being a low-carber, since in this case fat is not your enemy. Carbs are the enemy.

I have fried veggies, little fritters I make from almond flour, leftovers like cauliflower rice, leftover taco meat with a bit of cheese, and almond flour dough items. I've even fried the store-bought low-carb tortillas with some salt for guacamole and chips.

I've fried radishes, jicama, shredded veggies in dough, and kale.

Is it french fries? Of course not. But it turns out, if you get to eat a savory tasty salty warm something or other, it can be so satisfying. Just saying!

12. Size of bite

When cooking, think about what the finished item will be like on the fork as it's traveling to your mouth. Have you ever ordered a salad, and then you can barely eat it because it's heaped on the plate so precariously that the minute you dive in, it will drop things all over the table? Or the items are so big that once you load your fork, you can't really take a bite?

We talked briefly about this while we were talking about kale, but it works for many foods. When my daughter was little, her dad would make a literal crown of broccoli, and we jokingly referred to it as intimidating broccoli. I see this in restaurants also. Do you want a big hunk of broccoli, or do you want the cute nibbles of broccoli, ideally with a seasoning or sauce on them?

There is a reason why little kids like peas: they are so cute. Cut veggies and other ingredients into a nice size; it makes foods that you may not truly like to eat more approachable.

13. What to do when you are near the end of your daily carb budget

When you first start out, keeping to your daily carb budget may seem insurmountable. But considering the awesome benefits once you are through the knothole, it's worth it to stick to your goals and supplement with these very low-carb foods. If you are hungry and running out of grams for the day, eat more of these until you feel full. Because sensible keto means no suffering!

Zero grams

- 2 cups ground beef (or most any protein including fish)
- Butter
- Most lunchmeats
- Canned tuna (mix with mayo and celery!)
- 1 T minced fresh herbs like basil, cilantro, or parsley (great for dressings or as topper for most foods. Free nutrition!)
- ¼ cup hemp seeds (add to salads, yogurt bowls, and low-carb granolas)
- Canned sardines in oil (not as fishy as anchovies—toss with eggs, salad, or low-carb crackers)
- Mayo
- Some mustards

One-gram wonders

- 100 g shrimp
- 1 cup kale
- 2 eggs (consider mashing the yolks with salt and pepper to make deviled eggs!)
- 3 cups raw spinach
- 2 cups arugula
- 1/3 cup cabbage, shredded (think tacos!)
- ¼ cup sliced olives
- 2 oz spam, ham, or lunchmeat
- ¼ cup grated cheddar
- ¼ cup broccoli pieces
- 2 T crème fraiche
- ½ avocado
- 2 cups salad mix, shredded
- 5 spears of asparagus
- ½ small lemon
- 1 T fresh lemon juice
- 2 oz summer sausage (a generous slice of most brands)
- ½ cup cucumbers
- ½ cup celery
- 2 oz blue cheese
- 1/5 cup heavy whipping cream
- 1 cup fresh mushrooms (brown them crispy!)
- 1 cup swiss chard
- ½ cup zucchini
- 1/3 cup cauliflower
- 5 leaves radicchio (for wraps)
- 1 cup radicchio, shredded (for grilled veggie side)
- 1 ounce chia seeds (mix with heavy cream overnight in fridge to make pudding)
- ½ cup tofu (serve cold with unsweetened soy sauce, 1 t sesame oil, and fresh ginger)

Two grams

- 1-2 cheese stick(s) depending on brand
- 1 Boca burger and some Beyond Meat products
- 2 T almond butter
- 1 cup unsweetened almond milk
- ¼ cup raw almonds
- 1 ounce roasted pumpkin seeds
- 1 ounce serving of beef jerky

Three grams

- ¼ cup sour cream
- ½ cup broccoli
- ½ cup edamame beans with salt
- 2–3 ounce serving of fresh mozzarella (pair with olive oil, black pepper, and fresh basil ribbons)

Remember when we talked about knowing the difference between sprinting through a race versus having a marathon pace? I told you about how the third time was the charm for me, but the race was only beginning. To be successful for the long term, it helps to adopt a few strategies. The first is super simple because we as humans like to not go hungry. So here is my first tip for maintaining a marathon pace with your keto journey.

14. Be full—do not go hungry

The defining difference between keto and other eating philosophies is that on keto you should never be hungry. If you are hungry, you need to make a change. It often means that you are not eating enough at a time, or are not eating enough fat at a time, or are not eating enough times per day. It might also be that you are not in ketosis all the way.

We all grew up during a time when low fat was the way to prevent heart disease because Big Food wanted to protect their market for grainy, processed food. There is no market for Big Food if we start avoiding grains, because they are busy making us all kinds of snack foods to consume. Some say they created our bias against eating fat. I say quality fats are part of our diet, as our cave-dwelling ancestors ate all parts of the mammoth they caught.

Therefore, when I want to eat, I start with the idea of protein because it's simple to understand and provides a good bang for the buck. Proteins fill us up and provide the landscape for sauces. Then I think about what fat I can add to make it satisfying. Because what's not to like about being satisfied?!

Last, I try to sneak in some greens because greens are always good.

In the beginning, it might look like this:

Start a pan on medium heat with a generous amount of butter mixed with avocado oil. Coarsely chop a pile of spinach or "superfood greens" mix from the store. Fry until wilted with salt, reduce heat, and add eggs to bind it together. Optionally, throw in leftover meat from dinner or sliced avocado. Top with your favorite hot sauce, sour cream, and/or shredded cheese.

Or instead of eating hard-boiled eggs, what if you scooped out the yolks, added mayo, diced pickle, and mustard, or mashed with avocado and scooped it back into the whites? Deviled eggs are a better choice than hard-boiled eggs alone, and it's a bonus if you have leftover bacon from a prior day and can sprinkle that over the top.

Or what about starting a pan with diced shallots (which are lower-carb than onions), slice a favorite sausage or meat, and toss in a high-sided skillet. Add greens from the garden or a rough cut of frozen defrosted spinach, broccoli, or destemmed kale, add mushrooms if you like them and let them brown deeply, and then throw over a bowl of arugula, knowing the heat of the dish will wilt it just right?

The trick to making quick low-carb dishes is to set up your kitchen with needed items close to their point of use and to have the right staples on hand to quickly assemble something that tastes good.

The other trick is to think about what foods go together, so you can cook once but get more than one meal out of it. For example, if I'm planning to make tacos one week, I will make sure that either chili or spaghetti is also on the menu because I can brown the meat once for both dishes.

15. Yes, you can do this while traveling

I travel a lot for work, which also means eating out a lot or eating on planes. I also love to meet up with friends for happy hour. The trick to successfully eating out is to watch for things you can modify, so that in general you are eating what everyone else is eating. You also can eat before you go so you are less hungry, and for airplanes you can bring a bar or cheese plate on board.

Let's start at the top of the order. Bevvies . . .

Cocktails are better than wine because spirits are zero carb and you can mix them with soda water, lime or lemon, or even a mixer you bring from home like Zevia. However, a good food and wine pairing is valuable to me, so I will also drink wine but usually account for it by consuming fewer carbs the rest of the day. Most of all, moderation is key! Don't be that sloppy person we gotta carry out of the restaurant.

Then there are appetizers. Look for a charcuterie board, cheese plates, salad, sashimi-like tuna stacks, meatballs (estimating some bread crumbs, so they are not "free" of carbs but probably doable), hot artichoke, queso, guacamole, or onion sour cream dips, subbing celery sticks for dipping (or bringing a baggy of low-carb chips from home), unbreaded chicken wings, and buffalo cauliflower.

For entrées, look for chef's salad, chicken Caesar salad (hold the croutons, extra parm), any grilled meat with a side of vegetables, or even tacos—eating out the middle with a fork instead of eating the tortilla. Stay away from rice, beans, and corn, and don't be afraid to ask if they can modify a dish. Ask if they can add a side of avocado. I've eaten all over the world and find most everyone to be very accommodating. I even had the pleasure of a late night keiser-kreiner in Austria and just ate around the bun.

For dessert, ask for a side of strawberries or raspberries with heavy whipping cream or even develop a habit of not needing dessert at a restaurant. There are always those Curly Girlz sea salt caramels waiting for you back home . . .

On my last business trip, one of my co-workers couldn't believe that I ordered a wedge salad. Wedge salad is one of my favorite easy-to-find keto meals: it's lettuce, blue cheese, dressing, bacon, and sometimes crumbled egg or parsley.

Have you ever heard about the theory of self-limiting beliefs? Self-limiting beliefs are the words we say out loud that end up limiting our success because we buy into and believe the smaller belief. One of the most popular ones I hear is, "I can't do keto when traveling," or "Keto while traveling is impossible."

Let's shine a bright light of truth on that. What makes it hard?

Let's start with the airplane trip, since most business travel starts with a day in an airplane. Even if you are not on keto, do you really want to eat airplane food? No, you do not. Plan ahead and make sure you have food with you on the plane.

That can take so many forms.

If I know I'm traveling and I'm starting from home, I'll make a chicken salad sandwich on low-carb bread and throw it in my backpack with nuts, low-carb bars, cheese, chocolate, and low-carb gummy bears. Between that stash and the vodka on board, I am set.

Upon arrival, there is a wealth of restaurant staples that are low carb. Chicken wings, salads without croutons—especially my two faves, Caesar salad and wedge salad. Burgers without the bun. Crunchy brussels sprouts, omelets, hot artichoke dip with celery, buffalo wings, eating just the inside of a taco, avocado toast (eating just the tops not the bread), eggs and bacon, cauliflower dishes, and stews.

If you are at a conference with a lunch line, the themes are almost always taco bar, pasta bar, salad bar, or charcuterie board. For taco bar, create a pile of greens, add a meat on top, then add cheese, guac, and sour cream. Or for pasta bar, grab the salad greens up front, put the creamy pasta sauce on top, and go for any clear proteins, like meatballs (factoring in that it probably has some bread crumbs), any veggies, and skimming meats out of any sauces you see, especially cream sauce. Or, if there is a carved meat station, have them cut you a few pieces, and take the butter from the bread station to add needed fat.

Before you tell me why this won't work for you, I want to say that I work at a high-tech company in software sales. I have been to four years' worth of conferences and business trips, and there is always something to eat. I promise.

16. Yes, you can still go out with friends

Life is so wonderful. Part of wonderful is good times with good friends. No matter where they choose to eat, you can always find a protein with a veggie and have your modified cocktail. I encourage you to still go out and have fun with people. If where they want to go is truly a Guy Fieri-style diner dive with no options to modify, then just eat before you go. You can pick at something while you are with your friends, and you can have your 3–5 g in a glass of wine or choose my zero-carb cocktail approach.

I didn't beat cancer to have a life of no fun. I encourage you to have fun with your friends. Life is short and friendships are priceless!

17. Vacations and special occasions

You work hard. You deserve a break. When you spend your hard-earned money on a vacation, give yourself a break. After a year or more of being on keto, Alan and I went to Thailand for vacation. Considering how much I miss pad Thai noodles, I of course did not travel all the way to Thailand and not eat pad Thai. I ate pad Thai twice a day and probably took in a million carbs while I was there.

I hope to get to Thailand again someday but until then, this one week of my life did not ruin my keto journey. I ate it while I was there, marveling at how different and unique the experience was, and when we touched down a week later at SFO I went right back to eating keto. My body didn't miss a beat, and I didn't ruin the experience by entertaining any misgivings about carb consumption.

Special occasions are the same to me. Your best friend's wedding, your son's First Holy Communion, your cousin's baby shower. A meal here or there will not dramatically affect your keto life. The joy of time spent with family and friends will be forever treasured and will also make you a gracious guest. People will want to accommodate you, but you can encourage them that you will be fine. Part of the marathon pace is to be realistic about the sporadic and special times in your life and to enjoy them fully.

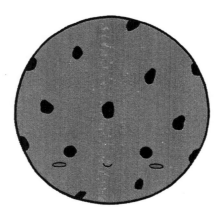

PRACTICE MAKES PERMANENT

When we were kids, if we wanted to win a race, we ran like crazy to get ahead even if we couldn't think through the length of the journey. As we got older, we learned to understand the difference between a sprint and a marathon pace.

The trick to staying in ketosis is to adopt a marathon pace. The trick to adopting a marathon pace is to understand and adopt the Pareto principle and to understand the difference between chasing and being.

The Pareto principle, aka the 80–20 rule, means that roughly 80% of the outcome comes from 20% of the causes, or in this case, the effort. It means that "good enough" can actually be good enough, and this knowledge can be what helps us keep going day after day. It's at the heart of why I'm writing this book. Striving for perfection can be a detriment if it causes us to want to give up. I want you to stick with it, and like all good things in life, your mindset will bless your effort.

Also, embracing the 80–20 rule means you understand that overthinking and trying to do things perfectly could freeze you into inaction. For example, of course I want to be the kind of person who makes their own keto taco seasoning, without fillers or other carb-contributing ingredients.

Some weeks, I find time and make my own (insert item here): taco seasoning, ketchup, mayo. Most of the time, as I mentioned, I cannot even find my car keys. In moments like that, remember that good-enough keto is better than giving up. Buy the store-bought taco seasoning, mayo, low-carb ketchup, etc. because the few added carbs are still better than going back to conventional high-carb eating.

18. Chasing vs. being

I love the daily emails from The SheFactor. I would have loved to have these daily pep talks at the beginning of my career, when I needed affirmation that my struggles were real and my intentions solid. This week's theme has been about how fashion can be an integral part of personal brand, and today's email subject line was "chasing vs. being." Although they were talking about chasing the latest craze in fashion, I want to talk about chasing vs. being as it relates to your keto journey.

The first thing I thought of when I saw that subject line was times in my life when I chased after a guy who really wasn't all that into me. Or chasing after the popular crowd at school or work when I wasn't bringing them anything of value. By pretending to be all things to all people, I was chasing after other people's validation instead of being who I truly am.

Do you feel me on this one?

From an early age, we mimic the sounds, gestures, and eye contact around us as a way to understand our world. As we grow, we join our tribe and assimilate. Ideally, somewhere in that journey we also discover our true north and find the balance between being in a community of like-minded people and still knowing who we are and being true to ourselves.

I am still on that particular journey.

Your experience of "chasing" may vary, but here is what I was reminded of. When I'm chasing after people, experiences, or things, it's actually a clue to me about what I really value. I'm chasing it because I want it. If I want it, what is that person/experience/thing/ attracting inside of me that makes me feel like I don't have it yet?

Let's go back to my chasing a guy example.

When I chased this particular guy, I really wanted him to like me and think I was cool. I imagined all the fun things we would do together and built up an amazing set of expectations that were not technically evident. It was my imagining about how it was going to go, and my types of imagining were indicative of what I thought was lacking in my life.

By wanting someone to think I was cool, maybe it was because I didn't think I was all that cool. By wanting to do fun things with someone, maybe it was because I wasn't making enough time in my schedule to do fun things with people I value. By wanting someone in my life at all, maybe it was because I was lonely. These are all gaps I could evaluate and decide if they are hints at what I value that is not in alignment with how I am living.

Fast forward to now. I now know I would not chase after someone to be my lover or friend. That is not because I'm suddenly amazing and have everything worked out. The main difference between then and now is that I've done a lot of work in the area of "being" me. I have spent time reducing the size of the gaps between my values and my way of living, which has increased my sense of self and my joy.

When it comes to my low-carb journey, I started out chasing after an ideal that my real life could not support. I was never going to cheat,

I was only going to eat organic and grass fed and local, and I was going to let food be my medicine.

In reality, in my true life of being me, I am a full-time working single mother, head of household, community volunteer, and frequent traveler. If I had chased after my image of how it had to be, I either would have gone crazy trying to make it be true despite the facts, or I might have given up. It takes more time and bandwidth than I currently have to achieve those goals.

Instead of chasing after the ideal that my lifestyle couldn't currently support, I asked myself what did I truly value, and what could reduce the gap. When I'm trying to deduce what I value and how my actions align, I love the magic of asking questions.

My inner dialogue went like this:

Why does it have to be all grass fed, all pastured, all ideal keto? Because I want to have the best possible outcome.

What does the best possible outcome look like? That I remain cancer-free for the rest of my life. That I keep this new unbloated belly I got while low-carbing.

Are you willing to give up the things that prevent you from doing it exactly as prescribed, like time spent traveling or community volunteering? No, I like those things.

If you like those things and want to keep low-carbing also, could you loosen up your definition of success so that you can accommodate both? Yes.

So what would a new definition look like? As long as I keep the bene-fits that I feel, especially around not being hungry all the time, feeling even and energetic, and knowing I'm not creating a good environ-ment for cancer cells, I would be happy with doing enough to keep these benefits.

What if you instead had a goal of making the best choices you can, given where you are at in every moment? If you are on an airplane, pick something that is low-carb without worry for grass fed and pastured.

The other interesting thing that happened with that inner mono-logue is I realized that I thought I wanted the flat belly, when in fact I wanted to be indifferent to food. I wanted the sustained energy and to not be a great place for cancer cells to grow.

Our joy in life is affected by the gaps in our life. The gaps between what we value and what we actually do or spend time on are what steals our joy. When you find yourself chasing, it's an invitation to consider what you want from that person/experience/thing that you don't already be/do/have. The gaps shrink the more we understand and align with our values, which happily is all within our control.

19. Give it two months to change your habits

Have you ever heard the story that if you do anything for 21 days it becomes a habit? In *Atomic Habits*, James Clear explains that it's actually closer to two months on average and can vary from 18 days to almost a year.

From James Clear: How Long it Really Takes to Build a New Habit

Phillippa Lally is a health psychology researcher at University College London. In a study published in the *European Journal of Social Psychology*, Lally and her research team decided to figure out just how long it actually takes to form a habit.

The study examined the habits of 96 people over a 12-week period. Each person chose one new habit for the 12 weeks and reported each day on whether or not they did the behavior and how automatic the behavior felt.

Some people chose simple habits like "drinking a bottle of water with lunch." Others chose more difficult tasks like "running for 15 minutes before dinner." At the end of the 12 weeks, the researchers analyzed the data to determine how long it took each person to go from starting a new behavior to automatically doing it.

The answer?

On average, it takes more than two months before a new behavior becomes automatic—66 days to be exact. And how long it takes a new habit to form can vary widely depending on the behavior, the person, and the circumstances. In Lally's study, it took anywhere from 18 to 254 days for people to form a new habit.

In other words, if you want to set your expectations appropriately, the truth is that it will probably take you anywhere from two to eight months to build a new behavior into your life—not 21 days.

Every Thursday, James shares 3 ideas, 2 quotes and 1 question in his 3-2-1 Thursday newsletter which has "the most wisdom per word of any newsletter on the web." Subscribe for free at JamesClear.com.

20. The holy grail of metabolic flexibility

I'll never forget the day I was out with my friend James Simzer, and he introduced me to the idea of metabolic flexibility. I had been low-carbing consistently for more than two years, and I was telling him about how when I went to Thailand, I just had to have pad Thai because I couldn't miss the chance to eat real Thai when in Thailand.

I mentioned that when I landed at SFO I remember being amazed that when I went right back to eating the way I always do at home, I didn't seem to go through any sort of keto flu or induction phase.

James explained to me that because I've been low-carbing for so long, my body is metabolically flexible. It knows how to use and con-vert fat, glucose, and glucose stores interchangeably, and therefore occasional carb consumption doesn't throw me under the bus.

Wait, What?!!!!

I was so excited because here is what this means to all of us. Once we become metabolically flexible, it means this is officially a way of life. It is sustainable. It is permanent.

Here is what I mean.

Think of your most favorite food ever, ideally one that is not accept-able on a low-carb diet. For me, that would be red velvet cupcakes with cream cheese frosting. I've tried to make them keto. No dice.

Do you have your favorite food item in your mind? Picture it in all its delicious glory.

Okay.

Now pretend you will never have that item ever again. Hard stop.

Doesn't work, right? Talk about a joy stealer!

I don't know about you, but I did not survive late-stage cancer to live a life without red velvet cupcakes! A brilliant life for me will always have an occasional cupcake.

Turns out, I can occasionally eat a red velvet cupcake, and I am still a low-carber. And this many years later my taste buds have naturally changed, and I cannot even eat a whole cupcake anymore anyway. I am truly satisfied eating just a few bites and calling it good.

I hear you thinking, "Not me! I could eat the whole batch!"

After you have low-carbed for four or more years, please write me and tell me what happened the day you ate the whole batch of your "favorite" thing. I tried it, and I got sick afterwards. I promise, if you stick with this way of eating for the long haul, you naturally will start to do things you previously thought unimaginable!

On the topic of eating at a friend's house

Once I became a low-carber, my friends started to worry about what to make for me when they hosted me for dinner. I always encouraged them not to worry and just make what they were going to make and that I'd find something to eat.

I am embarrassed to say that at first I didn't budge off my plan, and I ate only part of their meal, which made them feel bad that they missed the mark, and I was a bona fide poor guest. I put my need to be right ahead of my friend's need to be a gracious host.

I couldn't find the exact story to retell it here, but I recall while reading about Buddhism that there was a monk that went to a family's home with his young assistant, and the assistant was shocked that the monk ate the meat that the family served. What I recall most about the story was that the monk replied that it was more important to honor the efforts of the family in cooking the meal than to stand on principle just to be right. I really liked that story and starting doing that myself. When others cook for me, I eat what they make without comment. And I'm still keto.

I urge you to relax when you are in another person's home, to focus on what truly brought you all together, which is love. Anything made in love will be honored by love. You can get back to it when you get home.

This is how you make it permanent. This is real life.

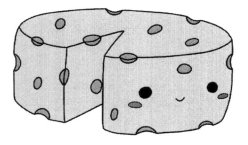

TECHNIQUES & RECIPES

My recipes are an approach and not an exact science.

I set out to write this book and tell the story of how to low-carb easily and permanently. I did not set out to write a cookbook.

But as I told friends what I was doing, they said things like, "Oh good, I want your spam fried rice recipe," or "Are you going to document how to make your desserts?"

What I found when trying to capture how I cook is that writing a cookbook with recipes that have exact measurements and well-described steps is a completely separate project. Not to mention, I cook by feel and not by measurement. I also prefer cookbooks with photos, don't you?

In the spirit of getting this book into your hands, I instead chose to include how I do things in case you would like to try making them. I'm a foodie who really loves to eat, so if you don't like to cook, be gentle with yourself as you try my methods.

The first part of this section is general techniques, and the second half is loosely how I make certain dishes that are popular with my posse.

If you would rather follow specific recipes, at the end of the book I've included a list of my favorite cookbook authors. These authors taught me how to adjust my cooking to be more in line with how I now want to eat, and they also solved some pretty important cravings I was having! They are amazing bloggers and authors who deserve your patronage.

Have you ever tried to follow someone else's recipe, and it just doesn't taste the same? To address that, I put any nuances to my approach in with each "recipe." I also post videos of me cooking in my kitchen, so find me on soc media or join my email list to stay connected.

Lastly, as I'm a busy mom, you will see that some of these recipes are actually just assembly of store-bought items. Per my 80–20 rule, I'd rather get good-enough food on the table than make it so unattainably perfect that I give up and hit a drive-through.

With all caveats aside, I present to you my techniques and recipes section!

21. Techniques

Browning things
Whether it's meat or veggies, I stir hardly at all, to help at least one side get crunchy and brown. For example, for ground meat, I sprinkle it evenly in the pan, crank the heat, and leave for many minutes until it has wept its liquid and reabsorbed it. I flip it in chunks like pancakes, leave it alone again, and then towards the end bust up the chunks and finish it. If you play with it more than that, the meat loses it's juices, doesn't reabsorb them, and gets tough.

With veggies, I similarly will stir hardly at all, which browns one side and wilts the other, which is usually sufficient. I like veggies to keep their bright color while softening enough to be yummy. Try it!

Let meat rest before slicing
Whether you've braised, grilled, or BBQed your favorite cut of meat, let it rest for five minutes before cutting it. Doing so will allow juices to reabsorb so that they don't run out all over your cutting board. Also, be sure to cut against the grain, which shortens the fibers in each bite.

Consider getting a sous vide
Long a staple in the restaurant trade, these amazing tools have come down in price and are now available for less than $100 on Amazon, or a little more at your favorite culinary store. Pronounced "sue-veed," this handy tool circulates water at the exact temperature needed, which means you get perfect results that are not overcooked. Your food item cooks inside a waterproof bag, and often it will come with an app with thousands of recipes you can follow.

For example, one of the easiest tricks to getting tender results with a chicken breast is to sous vide it for six hours at a lower temp than the 165°F normally required for food safety. Because of the longer cook time and the fact that the meat never exceeds the temperature you set, you get a tender result that everyone will ask how you achieved.

Freeze things flat
When I freeze things, I freeze them loose and flat so that I can bust off a piece anytime and not wait for a giant block of frozen food to defrost just to use some of it. For example, I like to buy a giant block of cheese and run it quickly through the grater on my Cuisinart for shredded cheese. To store it long term, I put some in a Ziploc in the fridge, but most goes into a gallon Ziploc in the freezer. I introduce a lot of air, pat pat pat it against my hand to make it as flat and loose as possible, and set it on the shelf of the freezer. Once frozen, you can let out the air and bust it up, and you will be able to keep it indefinitely and easily use it as you go.

Make your own bone and/or vegetable broths

After trimming and cutting vegetables, there are things you can compost like onion skins, spinach stems, celery tops, and herb stems. Instead, I add them to a gallon Ziploc that lives in my freezer, and when it's full I boil the contents with a few cups of fresh water to make vegetable broth.

Also, I like to either roast a whole chicken or buy a rotisserie chicken to shred meat from for quick tacos, chicken salad, and salad toppers. When the carcass is ready to toss, I put it in a pot with filtered fresh water and let it simmer for a few hours. You can do this with the veggies and get the base for your next soup creation, or freeze into an ice cube tray to use as a deglaze for pan sauces or as an ingredient for my no-cook tomato soup. I also freeze in one-cup portions for my tomato soup recipe.

A trick for eating quick

1. Brown a meat (which is usually low carb), deglaze pan with ½ cup of bone broth (also low carb), add 2 TB crème fraiche, serve over Palmini or other noodle sub.

   Example: brown sliced sausage, deglaze, add crème, serve to family over noodles, serve to self over zoodles, cauli rice, or mashed cauli, fat-style. Or brown bulk Italian sausage and add marinara, serve to family over spaghetti and serve to self over Palmini or zoodles. Or eat like a soup, adding crème to make it like a vodka sauce.

2. Start a pan with avocado oil on medium heat and add a handful of chopped veggies. Don't stir too much, get them to brown on one side. Reduce heat, add in dribs and drabs from other meals (leftover veggies, bits of bacon or taco fixings, that last bit of diced onion from the cutting board), and bind together with an egg or two. Salt and pepper to taste.

Recipes

Spam fried cauliflower rice

Serves 4

In the spirit of Hawaiian spam fried rice, I offer you this lower-carb version. If you truly cannot bear the idea of spam, you can sub ham or any leftover meat. Also, if you are in a hurry, I've had luck taking Asian-inspired ready-made (frozen) cauli rice and just adjusting seasonings for flavor (usually by adding more sesame oil).

<u>Ingredients</u>

1 can spam
Head of cauliflower
¼ white onion
2 stalks of celery
Duck fat
Avocado oil
2–3 eggs
¼ bunch of cilantro
Soy sauce
Sesame oil
Chili oil
Sriracha
Sesame seeds (optional)

<u>Directions</u>

1. Cut spam into half, half again, and half again, then cross cut to make cubes.
2. In 12" high-sided skillet, spread spam evenly on medium heat.

3. While waiting for it to brown, core cauliflower and grate using Cuisinart grating disc.
4. Stir once to flip spam onto other side, and use that time to dice onion and celery into small pieces.
5. Toss cauliflower, onions, and celery into pan, mix until combined. Add a duck fat puck and some avocado oil to lightly coat "rice."
6. Make a hole in middle of the mixture and crack in 2–3 eggs, stirring to scramble.
7. Mix whole dish together, adding in soy sauce, sesame oil, and chili oil to taste. Serve with drizzle of sriracha, chopped cilantro, and sesame seeds.

Nuances

At the end, taste it. If it needs more salt, add more soy sauce. If it tastes kinda flat, add more sesame oil. The component I add the most is usually more sesame oil, as it adds a nice rich flavor.

Try to get all components added before the cauliflower gets smooshy.

Adding cilantro (or fresh basil if you don't like cilantro) is important because herbs are nutrient dense.

Adding sesame seeds is optional. I just like them because they go with the dish and are an added source of good fats.

Variations

I have heard of making bacon fried rice instead of spam. I am too hapa for that.

You can use up veggies on hand like mushrooms, shishito peppers, and broccoli, or even bits of kale. It's a great dish to experiment with.

Tacos

<u>Ingredients</u>

1–2 lbs ground beef, ideally grass fed
Taco seasoning
Cabbage
Cilantro
Avocado
Cheese
Low–carb store-bought tortillas
Tortillas or shells for the rest of the fam

<u>Directions</u>

1. In a large high-sided skillet, crumble beef and leave without stirring on medium-high heat for five minutes or so. Sprinkle taco seasoning across the faceup raw side of the meat. While you wait (or prep other meal items) the meat will weep liquid, and if you wait long enough it will reabsorb, giving you a tastier outcome.
2. Visually divide pan into quarters and flip like a pancake. Use spatula and bust into small pieces.
3. Meanwhile, put tortillas into a clean dishtowel and heat for one minute in the microwave. You can also fry them, since fat is now your friend.
4. Create bowls to make a taco bar.

Everyone gets what they want, no worries!

Nuances

At the store you will see ground beef with different fat ratios. I like the one that is 80–20 because it crumbles nicely and is easy to break up the chunks. Leaner ground beef makes hard nuggets that are hard to transform into something good.

I've not had luck with those compressed bricks of grass-fed meat in plastic. I prefer loose ground meat in a grocery store butcher's Styrofoam tray.

Variations

Braise and brown pork shoulder to make carnitas tacos instead.

Make vegetarian by browning soyrizo instead of ground beef.

Tomato Soup

I like to serve this with grilled cheese sandwiches made from Franz Keto Bread and Lagunitas new Daytime IPA. Franz is zero net carb white sliced bread that can be found online and at Costco. Although tomatoes in quantity are high carb, due to portion size and net carb counts, this combination is a delicious reminder that there is life after keto!

Ingredients

1 28 oz can of San Marzano-style crushed tomatoes
1 cup broth, any flavor (can use the frozen one cup from your broth-making project)
¼ cup olive oil
½ small yellow onion
½ of a low-carb tortilla torn into pieces
1 tsp dried mushroom powder from Trader Joe's, or a handful of dried mushrooms (optional, adds umami. Even if you don't like mushrooms you will like this!)
1 T Bragg's nutritional yeast flakes (optional, adds umami)
1 tsp salt
½ tsp pepper
1 tsp Italian seasoning or mix of dried basil and oregano, to taste

Directions

1. Load all ingredients in listed order into Vitamix or blender and blend until completely smooth, about 7 minutes. With a Vitamix, after seven minutes on high the soup will be warm enough to serve immediately.
2. Top each serving with drizzle of olive oil, more salt and pepper to taste, and chiffonaded herbs from the garden, such as

basil and parsley. As a variation, top with crème fraiche and fresh chopped chives.

3. This is a very filling soup, so you will have leftovers unless you have more than 6–8 people over.

Homemade creamy dressing

I love making this with a wide range of cheeses. It makes a delicious creamy dressing that satisfies! You also can make it a Green Goddess dressing by adding in an extra handful of favorite garden herbs. Lasts a week in the fridge.

Ingredients

¼ c sour cream
¼ c mayo
2 oz crumbled gorgonzola or other preferred cheese (try cotija, feta, or parmesan)
2 T cilantro, parsley, tarragon, or other fresh herb
Heavy whipping cream, to thin to desired consistency

Directions

1. Assemble and combine all ingredients. Store in fridge for up to a week.

Homemade Thai peanut dressing

I love this dressing on salads, on chicken, or as a dipping sauce for Asian-inspired fried treats. It is reminiscent of the dipping sauce you get with fresh spring rolls. Toss it with cabbage, shredded chicken, and herbs like cilantro or basil, and trust me, it's the bomb.

Ingredients

¼ c balsamic vinegar, pick a lower-than-average-carb version
2 T allulose or monk fruit sweetener (alternative to white sugar)
2 T brown Swerve (alternative to brown sugar)
2 T soy sauce or coconut aminos
½ t dried crushed red pepper flakes
1 clove garlic, pressed
2 T peanut butter, pick a lower-carb version
½ c chopped cilantro (or if you really don't like it, sub fresh
      basil leaves)
2 T chopped fresh mint
Handful of crushed peanuts (optional)

Directions

1. Melt everything except greens and peanuts in a pot and remove from heat as soon as it starts to boil.
2. Stir in greens (and peanuts, if desired).

Mashed Cauliflower

Ingredients

Cauliflower, whole head
½ to full stick of salted butter (I like the whole stick, you might like less), grass fed if you can find it
Heavy cream or equivalent
Salt and pepper to taste

Directions

1. Cut head of cauliflower in half, remove stem.
2. Bust into large florets (chunks) to fit into steamer. Steam until just fork tender.
3. Drain and place into food processor work bowl or blender.
4. Working in batches, whirl cauliflower with part of the butter and part of the cream. It doesn't matter if each batch is slightly different because in the end we will stir it all together. The goal is hot cauliflower that melts butter and just enough cream so that it combines together into a mash.
5. Add each batch to a large bowl as you go, and at the end stir it all together, adding salt and pepper to taste.

Nuances

I salt and pepper each batch by gut feel so that I have less to do at the end. As long as you are not too heavy-handed with each batch, at the end it's just adding a bit more.

Variations

Make cheesy by blending in shredded parmesan or grated cheddar.

Make twice-baked by blending in cream cheese, cheddar cheese, and baking for 20 minutes at 350°F. This is especially effective when using frozen riced cauliflower in steam bags to disguise the frozen veggie taste. I sometimes rinse after cooking and press out water in a sieve to make drier crumbles.

Make non-dairy by subbing in ghee for the butter and other dairy for the cream and cheese.

Use this mash on top of gravy, meat, and veggies for shepherd's pie.

Fry leftover mash and top with eggs for breakfast.

Chili

Ingredients

1 lb ground beef, ideally grass fed
1 bulb of shallot, diced
1 package taco or chili seasoning mix
1 can Eden Foods black soybeans (not regular black beans), drained
1 can crushed tomatoes

Directions

1. Brown beef in a large high-sided skillet.
2. When most of the pink is gone, add the shallots.
3. When the shallots are translucent (about 3 min), add taco seasoning, beans, and tomatoes.
4. Stir and serve!

Nuances

Shallots are lower-carb than onions, but if you can't find them, onion is okay in my book. Although it is higher in carbs than other vegetables, normally you don't eat a lot in one sitting.

This is a dish you can make for you and your nonparticipating family by serving their portions over rice.

<u>Variations</u>

Make a chop sauce of diced white onion, cilantro, and lime, and use as a topping.

Top with shredded cheese.

Add cut up grass-fed hot dogs.

Spaghetti sauce

Ingredients

1 lb bulk Italian sausage
1 jar of marinara
Shredded parmesan or Italian mixed cheeses like asiago, mozzarella, and Romano
Your choice of noodle substitute

Directions

1. Start pot of boiling water if making pasta for the rest of the family.
2. Spread sausage evenly around a 12″ high-sided skillet and turn flame to medium-high.
3. Leave undisturbed in pan until it is fragrant and browned on one side. Flip sections of sausage one at a time and leave alone until browned.
4. Using the edge of a spatula, bust up the sections to reveal any pink parts that still need browning.
5. Once most of the pink is gone, pour entire jar of marinara on top. Cover and finish working on pasta for rest of family and your own noodle substitute.

Nuances

Double this recipe to have leftovers or to feed more than 4–6 people.

If using canned Palmini noodles, boil them in a small saucepan with water for ten minutes.

When selecting marinara, look at all the labels and choose the lowest carb one (usually 6 g carb per ½ cup).

Noodle substitute suggestions

You can put this sauce on top of an omelet or on top of zoodles or spaghetti squash.

If you have not had a lot of carbs in a day, I really like to splurge on Carba-Nada noodles.

Low-carb gnocchi https://www.ibreatheimhungry.com/fathead-keto-gnocchi-low-carb/

Variation: I have always liked pink vodka sauce and don't know how they make it. I stir a tablespoon of heavy cream into my personal bowl and like how it reminds me of that sauce.

Lasagna

<u>Ingredients</u>

1 carton ricotta
1 egg
1 t Italian seasoning blend (basil, oregano)
1 package low-carb tortillas
1 package shredded mozzarella
1 jar of marinara or a batch of my spaghetti sauce with sausage

<u>Directions</u>

1. Preheat oven to 350°F.
2. Stir together ricotta, egg, and seasoning. Set aside.
3. In a tall, round casserole dish, make layers as follows:
   Sauce, tortilla, ricotta, shredded cheese, sauce
4. Add next tortilla, pushing down on all layers to compress.
   Repeat.
5. Continue on until one inch from top of dish, ending with
   shredded cheese. Cover with foil and bake until bubbly.

<u>Nuances</u>

This dish is much better a day ahead. I usually make it, bake it, let it cool, and refrigerate overnight. In the morning it's easy to slice and pack for lunch.

<u>Variation</u>

Substitute eggplant slices for the tortillas.

Chanterelles and eggs

When I was younger I didn't like mushrooms, but I did like chanterelles. Even if you don't like mushrooms, I hope you will try this dish!

Ingredients

2T butter
1 pkg chanterelles (or if buying in bulk, a heaping handful)
6 eggs
2T heavy cream, half and half, or milk
Salt and pepper to taste

Directions

1. Brush chanterelles to remove debris. Do not rinse in water!
2. Slice into ¼-inch slices.
3. Melt butter into large fry pan and fry chanterelles gently on medium heat until lightly browned. Add more butter as necessary if they absorb it, you want the pan to be a bit oily.
4. In separate bowl, whisk eggs with milk, salt, and pepper.
5. Reduce heat and add eggs. If you like custardy eggs, reduce heat to very low and stir constantly. Otherwise, leave at low/med and scramble as desired. Serve immediately.

Chef John's Coq Au Vin

This is my favorite chicken recipe, and it goes great with mashed cauliflower. It's so delicious on a rainy night, is easy to do, and guests love it. From allrecipes.com

Ingredients

6 bone-in, skin-on chicken thighs
1 pinch kosher salt and freshly ground black pepper to taste
8 oz bacon, sliced crosswise into ½-inch pieces
10 large button mushrooms, quartered
½ large yellow onion, diced
2 shallots, sliced
2 t all-purpose flour (it's okay, it's going to be split six ways), or substitute carbalose flour
2 T butter
1½ cups red wine
6 sprigs fresh thyme
1 cup chicken broth

Directions

1. Preheat oven to 375°F.
2. Season chicken thighs all over with salt and black pepper.
3. Place bacon in a large ovenproof skillet and cook over medium-high heat, turning occasionally, until evenly browned, about 10 minutes. Transfer bacon with a slotted spoon to a paper towel-lined plate, leaving drippings in the skillet.
4. Increase heat to high and place chicken, skin side down, into skillet. Cook in hot skillet until browned, 2–4 minutes per side. Transfer chicken to a plate; drain and discard all but 1 tablespoon drippings from the skillet.

5. Lower heat to medium-high. Sauté mushrooms, onion, and shallots with a pinch of salt in the hot skillet until golden and caramelized, 7–12 minutes.
6. Stir flour and butter into vegetable mixture until completely incorporated, about 1 minute.
7. Pour red wine into the skillet and bring to a boil while scraping browned bits of food off the bottom of the pan with a wooden spoon. Stir bacon and thyme into red wine mixture; simmer until wine is about reduced, 3–5 minutes. Pour chicken broth into wine mixture and set chicken thighs into skillet; bring wine and stock to a simmer.
8. Cook chicken in the preheated oven for 30 minutes. Spoon pan juices over the chicken and continue cooking until no longer pink at the bone and the juices run clear, about 30 minutes more. An instant-read thermometer inserted into the thickest part of the thigh, near the bone, should read 165°F (74°C). Transfer chicken to a platter.
9. Place skillet over high heat and reduce pan juices, skimming fat off the top as necessary, until sauce thickens slightly, about 5 minutes. Season with salt and pepper; remove and discard thyme. Pour sauce over chicken.

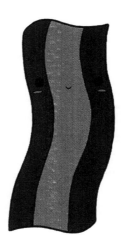

Pizza

After all this talk about having the hookup for pizza, I'd better give you my fave tips for dealing with pizza cravings. It can start simply: just buy the frozen pizzas from Real Good Foods, which has both chicken crust and cauliflower crust, both good for different reasons and easy to find. I also have a couple of versions I like to make on my own. One is a cauliflower crust, and one uses the magic mozzarella dough from Carolyn Ketchum.

Dough #1: Cauliflower crust pizza

2 ½ c grated cauliflower (about a half a head, run through box grater or Cuisinart with grating disc)
1 egg, lightly beaten
1 ¼ c shredded mozzarella
2 T parmesan
Salt and pepper to taste

Directions

1. Preheat oven to 425°F.
2. Bake cauliflower for 15 min to partially cook and dry it out, or microwave it in a large glass work bowl for 6–8 min on high. Squeeze out all the moisture in a clean, dry dishtowel, and dump into a dry work bowl.
3. Mix dried, cooked cauliflower with the egg, cheeses, and salt and pepper.
4. Pat into a 10" circle on a Silpat or parchment. Spray top lightly with avocado oil and bake 10–15 min or until golden.
5. Top with sauce and desired toppings. Bake again until bubbly.

Dough #2: Magic mozzarella dough by Carolyn Ketchum

This dough is amazing and can be used in sweet recipes by substituting 1 t vanilla extract for the garlic powder and adding ¼ c of allulose or erythritol with the almond flour in step 4.

Ingredients

6 oz by weight pre-shredded part-skim mozzarella cheese (about 1.5 cups, weigh on food scale for best outcome)
3 T butter or ghee
½ cup almond flour
¼ cup coconut flour
2 t baking powder
½ t garlic powder
¼ t salt
1 egg

Directions

1. Preheat oven to 350°F.
2. Sprinkle large Silpat or parchment with almond flour.
3. In large saucepan, melt cheese and butter over low heat until it can be combined.
4. Remove from heat and add flours, baking powder, garlic powder, egg, and salt.
5. Turn dough out onto floured work surface and knead to combine, which should only take about a minute. If it's still sticky, add a bit more almond flour.
6. To make crust, roll between two pieces of parchment or wax paper until circle is 12".
7. Bake at 350°F for 10–15 minutes or until golden. Add your fave toppings and bake for another 5–10 minutes or until bubbly.

Overnight Keto Mac and Cheese

Based on Ina Garten's famous overnight mac and cheese, this is a medium-carb joy bringer that I just had to include as an incentive to get past the six-month mark. For any long term low-carber, this is easy to fit into your goals. The whole 13x9 pan is 80 grams of carbs, so you can get from 6–10 grams per serving and will feel like you had an amazing treat. I served this with the braised short rib recipe in the Joule app (which also takes 24 hours), and it was better than any fancy restaurant meal. Best of all, I didn't have to cook the night I served both these dishes, as you do most of the work the day before.

Ingredients

1 bag of al dente Carba-Nada brand noodles
2 t salt
1 t pepper
3 cups heavy cream
2 cups grated gruyere (use Cuisinart grating discs to make short work of both cheeses)
1 cup grated sharp white cheddar (I buy the big Tillamook block and use the freezer bag trick from my tips section)
¼ t ground nutmeg
2 T melted butter, plus extra to butter the dish
3 slices toasted Franz Keto bread

Directions

1. The day before serving, boil the noodles for three minutes and drain.
2. While pasta is cooking, in medium saucepan warm the cream, nutmeg, 1 cup of the gruyere, ½ cup of the cheddar, salt, and pepper over low heat, stirring occasionally. Cook until cheeses are fully melted.

3. Add drained pasta to the crème mixture. Cover and refrigerate overnight. The pasta will absorb the cream mixture and expand.
4. An hour before serving, let mixture come to room temp. Preheat oven to 400 degrees.
5. Butter 13x9" pan and spread mixture evenly. Sprinkle the remaining cheeses on top.
6. In Cuisinart or blender, turn the toasted bread into crumbs and blend in the 2 T melted butter. Sprinkle on top of cheese.
7. Cover with foil and bake for 15–20 minutes until bubbly, rotating halfway through. Uncover during last few minutes of baking, being careful not to burn the breadcrumbs. Serve hot. Sing my praises and leave me a glowing Amazon review. I made that last part up. Enjoy!

Snowball cookies

This recipe from Brenda Bennett of sugarfreemom.com is a crowd-pleaser because it's not only keto but also paleo, gluten-free, and vegan! Every time I bring these cookies to a party, no one can believe they are low carb. They are singlehandedly the marketing poster child for keto.

Ingredients

1 stick Earth Balance buttery sticks (or butter)
1 ½ c almond flour
1 c pecans, chopped
½ c powdered allulose, monk fruit, or Swerve
1 t vanilla extract
½ t vanilla liquid stevia
¼ t salt
Extra powdered Swerve or other sweetener to roll the cookies in

Directions

1. Process all ingredients in a food processor until the batter forms a ball. Taste the batter and adjust sweetener and salt.
2. Using a cookie scoop if you have it or spoons if not, make 24 balls.
3. Freeze for 20–30 min and toward end of that time, preheat oven to 350°F.
4. Bake 15 min or until golden around edges. While baking, prep a bowl with powdered sugar of choice.
5. Let cookies rest out of oven for a few minutes, but as soon as they can be handled without falling apart, roll in the powdered goodness to create snowballs.
6. When cool, store in an airtight container.

Rum cake

These is an assembly recipe rather than an actual recipe!

<u>Directions</u>

1. Purchase the vanilla cake mix from Swerve or any of the Sweet Logic cake mixes.
2. I really like nuts in my rum cake, Tortuga-style. If you want nuts, grab a handful of walnuts or pecans, coarsely chop, and scatter on the bottom of the cake pan. I use a Silpat cake form, but if you are using a regular pan be sure to grease it before scattering the nuts.
3. Take ¼ cup of brown sugar substitute (Swerve or Lakanto) and scatter in with the nuts.
4. Make the cake as directed. You can sub some of the water in the mix with rum. I like Cruzan brand clear white rum, but any rum you like is good! Pour half of the batter into the pan, add more brown sugar substitute and nuts, and pour in the rest of the batter.
5. While the cake is baking, make a syrup with half a stick of butter and your favorite low-carb sweetener (my new fave is the allulose clear syrup from Wholesome) and rum to taste.
6. When the cake is done baking, poke holes all over and pour the syrup over the top.

Kimber's riff on Marilyn's cheesecake

I am so grateful to Tina and Melinda for sharing grandma Marilyn's original cheesecake recipe with me. Imagine a lemony delicious cheesecake with a sour cream top! This is my somewhat keto version, offered in honor of an amazing set of women!

Ingredients

Crust
¼ c melted butter
2–3 c finely crushed nuts

1ˢᵗ layer
3 large or 6 small packages Philly cream cheese
¾ c powdered allulose, monk fruit, or Swerve
3 eggs, mix in one at a time
1 squeezed lemon (but I put in way more)
1/3 t vanilla extract

2ⁿᵈ layer
1 pint sour cream
½ c allulose, Swerve, or monk fruit (anything that says it measures cup for cup with regular sugar)
1/8 t vanilla

Directions

1. Combine crust ingredients. Spread in deep pie pan but don't bake yet.

2. Combine all 1st layer ingredients and pour over nut crust. Bake for 30 minutes at 325°F.
3. Combine all 2nd layer ingredients and spread over cheesecake. Bake at 475°F for exactly 5 minutes.

23. Cookbooks I love

When I wrote this book, I learned that those who went before me with detailed and tested recipes are a different breed. I applaud the amount of time it must have taken to make their beautiful cookbooks. The following people made my journey easy and delicious, and I'd like to thank them here by encouraging all of you to try their recipes!

Maria Emmerich is the most technical author I follow, and if you want to understand the science of keto over time, her many books will satisfy those of you that need research and science. In addition, if you want to do an intense "cleanse" type approach to go hard in the beginning, check out her book *The 30-Day Ketogenic Cleanse*, which has many tasty recipes and resets your metabolism for a fast start to keto.

Carolyn Ketchum is the mastermind behind *All Day I Dream About Food,* which is one of the most popular low-carb, gluten-free blogs on the web. Her beautifully illustrated cookbook *The Everyday Ketogenic Kitchen* is a joy to read and filled with attainable and delicious recipes for everyday living. She's incredibly creative, which speaks to my desire for baked goodies and heartwarming comfort foods.

Mellissa Sevigny is the creative force behind the popular food blog *I Breathe, I'm Hungry.* She focuses on low-carb and gluten-free recipes, and everything she makes is so delicious! Her cookbook *Keto For Life* has everything from easy low-carb marinara sauce and 5-minute Alfredo sauce to homemade kefir, spicy tuna cakes, and an epic cream cheese frosting. She's the pioneer for Sensible Keto because she's good at food but is busy like anyone, so her style is approachable and real.

Megha Barot and **Matt Gaedke** are the power couple behind the incredibly popular website KetoConnect.net. They are the masters of learning to create healthier versions of their favorite dishes, and their videos are entertaining and educational. They taught me to reframe favorite recipes and how to meal prep on the weeks I'm up for it. Their cookbook *Keto Made Easy* has fun recipes for both savory and sweet cravings.

Thank you all for making my journey delicious and satisfying!

24. Brand review

New companies are launching all the time, so stay current by downloading my *Sensible Keto Companion Guide* at ketokimber.com!

Candies

- Curly Girlz for their chocolate and caramel candies. You can even get a Valentine's Day box filled with candies you would never guess were low-carb. They even have fudge for the holidays!
- Smart Sweets—do you miss fruity, chewy candies like gummy bears? Smart Sweets was started by Tara Bosch, and she has gummies, Swedish fish, and sour patch-type candies nailed!
- Lily's—I loved them even when all I could find was their chocolate chips in the baking aisle, and I love them even more for their many flavors of candy bars as well as milk and dark chocolate versions of peanut butter cups!
- ChocZero—has many delicious bars including rare flavors like raspberry and salted almond. I like that the bars are thin and easy to bite into.
- The yellow box Chocorite has many chocolate bars and a favorite rice crispy caramel coated in chocolate!

Baking mixes

- Swerve cake mixes—they have chocolate, which I embellish with low-carb chocolate chips and homemade frosting. They also have a vanilla cake, which is great with berries and cream on top, or you can take it in a different direction by adding rum and nuts and finishing with melted butter and cinnamon.

- Diabetic Kitchen brownie mix—brownies, need I say more? I also love their doughnut mix, which I parbake and then fry and dredge in allulose. Malasadas, move aside!
- Primal NOMs mug cake—available in so many flavors and available as a monthly subscription. I especially like the pumpkin spice and the lemon but can also do chocolate, mocha, carrot cake, and more!
- KNOW foods—an original that makes mixes but you can also buy chocolate chocolate chip cupcakes already made, waffles, marshmallows (paired with butter and low-carb cereal for your own Krispy treats!), maple syrup, ketchup, and big bags of mini chocolate chips.

Bread and related

- KNOW foods
- Mission brand low-carb tortillas
- Tortilla Factory wheat and white low-carb tortillas
- Cali'flour Foods sandwich thins, pizza shells, crackers, and freezer goods
- Diabetic Kitchen granolas. My favorite is their almond butter granola with heavy whipping cream. So delicious!
- The Cereal School—low-carb old-school cereal flavors from when we were kids!
- Magic Spoon low-carb cereals

Prepped foods

- Quest pizza
- Real Good Foods premium ice cream, pizza, enchiladas, and breakfast sandwiches
- Lakanto pancake and waffle mix, sugars, and maple syrup
- Nekstella chocolate hazelnut spread and syrup
- NuNaturals NuStevia pourable chocolate syrup

Online food sellers

- Vitacost—especially for Eden Foods black soybeans
- Netrition—especially for breads and chips
- Amazon

Subscriptions

- Keto Krate—a wonderful way to not only send a signal to the market that we need more low-carb options but also to support new companies that use KK as their launch platform. With each box you get a range of products to try as well as deals toward your first orders from the new companies.
- Hamama—adding microgreens to your food adds nutrition in a delightful way. This can be less intimidating than a huge plate of veggies, is more potent, and looks nice on the plate. It's also fun to watch them grow. They are so easy, they will show you that you DO in fact have a green thumb!
- Sweet Logic mug cakes—five packets per shipment that you can mix and match depending on your mood.

**This list changes all the time, and some of these companies have deals for my readers. Visit ketokimber.com to get your free copy of the *Sensible Keto Companion Guide*, which includes a lifetime of free updates! Yay!

25. Call to action: join my community

Now that you've read my book, consider joining my community! My community is not just for eating keto, it's actually about what we can each do today to become a better version of our best selves. As I learn things that I find useful, I like to share my findings with all of you!

To join my community, go to **ketokimber.com** and subscribe to my mailing list.

Once subscribed, you'll get your free *Sensible Keto Companion Guide*, which contains all the links and companies I recommend in this book and new ones as I become aware of them. It's a handy guide that I will update and send to my subscribers regularly, including some special deals just for you!

Some of the techniques in this book are just better to watch in person. Visit me on my blog to watch my tutorials on browning, sous vide, and more. I take requests, and I love to convert conventional favorites to keto, so let me know what you'd like to see next!

with pure joy!

EAT WELL - LIVE JOYFULLY - LOVE EVERY MOMENT

WITHPUREJOY.COM

Photo credit: Sharon Hoyt
www.sharonhoytphotography.com
www.beautycounter.com/sharonhoyt

I love to eat. I always have. I love farm-to-fork restaurants, good wine, good times with friends, and traveling abroad. I also love being healthy, which in my life has ranged from low fat to vegetarian and raw vegan, paleo, and gluten-free. But the one thing that has turned out to be the most delicious and easiest to do is low-carbing for the long run. I call it Sensible Keto for short. "Keto" is a charged word for some, and I urge you to give my sensible version a chance. Sensible keto is low carb, medium protein, and high fat; and in my world, quality counts. I prefer grass-fed and pastured meats when I can, and hitting the farmers market, and eating things as close as possible to their natural state (not heavily processed).

I also am a late-stage cancer survivor who likes life, and since I am a kid at heart, I also am a sucker for sea salt caramels, In-N-Out burgers, and gummy bears, which are generally NOT found in nature. I am your maven if you want to get the advantages of keto while still having some fun. Because yes, I still don't know where the car keys went.

THANK YOU for reading my book!

This is my first book, and I never thought I'd be an author. I really want to make keto accessible and delicious for as many seekers as possible.

Please consider leaving me a helpful review on Amazon so that I can help others find this style of keto.

Gratitude!